THE DANCE PROGRAM

A Series of Publications in Dance and Related Arts

Volumes in Preparation

The Bennington Years: 1934-1942, a comprehensive history, chronology, and source book, by Sali Ann Kriegsman

The Art and Practice of Ballet Accompanying (in two volumes), by Elizabeth Sawyer

The Ballet Russe (in four volumes), edited by George Jackson

Imperial Dancer, a biography of Felia Doubrovska, by Victoria Huckenpahler

Antony Tudor, a biography, by Fernau Hall

Dancer's Diary, by Dennis Wayne, *introduction by Joanne Woodward*

Marius Petipa: Materials, Reminiscences, Articles, edited by A. Nekhendzi, *translated from the Russian by Tamara Bering Sunguroff*

Handbook of Television Dance, by Richard Lorber and Peter Grossman

Jean Cocteau and the Ballet, by Frank W. D. Ries

Memoires d'un Bourgeois de Paris, by Dr. Louis Véron (originally published in 1856), *translated from the French by Victoria Huckenpahler*

Les Petits Mystères de l'Opéra, by Albéric Second (originally published in 1844), *translated from the French by Victoria Huckenpahler*

Dance as Art, by Curtiss Carter

In Search of Béjart, by Pamela Gaye

Speaking of Dance, by Lee Stern

The International Bibliography of Labanotated Dance Works and Other Movement Scores, by Mary Jane Warner

The Mask in Modern Theatre, by Barbara Lecker

Bel Canto Opera, by Mary Jane Matz

KATHERINE DUNHAM
A Biography

Katherine Dunham *(photo by Raymond Voinquel—used with permission of the Dance Collection of the New York Public Library)*

KATHERINE DUNHAM

A Biography

Ruth Beckford

Foreword by Arthur Mitchell

MARCEL DEKKER, INC.   NEW YORK & BASEL

Library of Congress Cataloging in Publication Data

Beckford, Ruth.
  Katherine Dunham, a biography.

  (The Dance program ; v. 14)
  Includes index.
  1. Dunham, Katherine. 2. Dancers–United
States–Biography. 3. Choreographers–United
States–Biography. I. Series.
GV1785.D82B4   793.3'2'0924   [B]   79-4577
ISBN 0-8247-6828-0

MARCEL DEKKER, INC.
270 Madison Avenue, New York, New York 10016

Current printing (last digit):
10 9 8 7 6 5 4 3 2 1

PRINTED IN THE UNITED STATES OF AMERICA

*Dedicated to the loving memory
of
Mama, Daddy, and my brother, Beck*

I would like to thank the following friends for their support and help on this book: Katherine Dunham, Maya Angelou, Vévé Clark, Arthur Mitchell, Jeanelle Stovall, Roy Thomas, Marian Van Tuyl, Giovannella Zannoni, and special thanks to my husband, Cero.

Foreword

Katherine Dunham's contribution to American dance cannot be too highly valued. She has always been and remains a germinal force in our tradition of theatrical dance. Without her persuasive influence as stellar performer, choreographer, anthropologist, and educator, American dance, now so rich and varied, would certainly present a much leaner profile.

As a researcher, Dunham went to the virgin sources to gather material, which with astonishing genius she translated into theater pieces that communicated expressively without distorting or vulgarizing the original.

As an educator, she counseled and inspired while developing a deeply thought-out and viable technique of moving. Every choreographer and dancer working today owes her a profound debt of gratitude.

Katherine Dunham was a pioneer in the truest sense of the word, and the fruits of her journeys and settlements are engraved in our heritage as dancers and people.

Arthur Mitchell
Director
Dance Theatre of Harlem

Contents

Illustrations

Introduction

"E—E—E—E—E push, in out, in out," Miss Dunham said in a quiet voice over the sound of the quivering beat played by her congo drummers. Wow! I was actually in her company, attending my *first* class before my *first* rehearsal!

"Keep your heels flat," Miss Dunham said. She corrected me, never raising her voice (but I knew never to make the same mistake twice). It didn't take me long to know that "E—E—E—E—E" meant "get ready," or the more common dance term, "and" (properly spelled *Y* in Haitian *patois*).

Mama, sitting on a bench with her back straight against the wall, held her head proud and high. The company dancers, Tommy Gomez, Laverne French, Roger Ohardieno, Claude Marchant, Talley Beatty, Lavinia Williams, Syvilla Fort, Lucille Ellis, and Janet Collins, were all busy practicing the Dunham technique that I was trying to learn in one session. At the time I didn't realize the influence it would have on my future dance career and my life.

My early dance training had consisted of fourteen years with Florelle Batsford at her studio of ballet, tap, and acrobatics in Oakland, California. Along with these dance forms, my classes had included Spanish, hula, baton, toe tap, toe acrobatics, and an assortment of novelty numbers. Since classes weren't common in the thirties and forties, I had studied privately and had excelled in toe tap and toe acrobatics lessons, which were reserved for Batsford's advanced students. Today they're lost dance forms. (Toe tap shoes had round metal taps attached to regular toe shoes; on these metal discs a regular tap routine could be danced. Toe acrobatic shoes had round rubber soles glued onto the point of regular toe shoes. The regular contortions of acrobatics were performed while landing and taking off from the points of the toe shoes.)

I had first seen Miss Dunham acting, dancing, and singing as Georgia Brown at San Francisco's Curran Theater in *Cabin in the Sky*, starring Ethel Waters. After a matinee, Mama and I went backstage to Dunham's dressing room where she invited me to show my routine.

Mama had always said, "All you can do is your best." In my excitement I got into a costume Mama had made. Then Miss Dunham led me on the stage and summoned her entire company and some cast members to sit in the audience and watch. Accompanying myself with round metal discs on my fingers, I performed an acrobatic finger cymbal dance consisting of splits, flips, bends, and stretches, all done in slow motion to show strength, control, and a sense of rhythm.

Miss Dunham and her company congratulated me on my performance, and I was accepted into the company.

The next day I got leave from Oakland Technical High School and, gathering my leotard and tights from home, took my first Dunham class. I became a "Dunham Dancer."

"E—E—E—E—E, body roll up, two, three, four."

Ever since that day in 1943 we have been friends.

After being accepted into the company, I went to San Francisco for a three-week indoctrination. Each morning I studied Dunham technique and each afternoon repertoire. Since Miss D always traveled with at least three complete shows, the challenge was tremendous. I can remember moving my feet to rehearse a new step while sitting on the "C" Key System train during my daily commute from Oakland.

Many times the dances we learned used vocal accompaniment. One of the songs contained the beautiful Haitian lyric, *Congo Ibo Lele-O Ouayho, Ouayho!* Although the Haitian word–sounds were strange, I learned to sing them correctly, and to sing in other foreign languages. Not only were the songs unusual, but also the new style of movement, which was "primitive," or simply Dunham technique.

Because I was the youngest and newest member of the company, I was graciously given help by everyone. Miss D herself was always patient, giving instructions and corrections in a calm, encouraging manner. I definitely wanted to please her. I was determined to be good.

After three weeks of intensive work I was ready for the tour. The tour was to proceed from San Francisco to Canada, then return to San Francisco. Miss D also invited Mama to go. (I'm certain it was because I was a young, naive-looking teenager, but I was grateful, and Mama became the "mother" of the company.)

The tour was a series of "firsts" for me. It was my first time to leave California and the United States, and to see snow falling. It was also my first time on a ship, and to give autographs. It included too many firsts to mention, but each one remains a fond memory.

At the end of six weeks Mama allowed me to make the decision either to remain with Miss D and sign a seven-year contract, as she had invited me to do, or leave the company, finish high school, and attend the University of California at Berkeley, which had been my previous plan. The decision was hard to make. I had enjoyed every minute of the tour, and from San Francisco the company was bound for Hollywood to make the movie *Stormy Weather*. I wanted to do the movie, but I also remembered that my parents, Felix and Cora Beckford, had always stressed education. I was the youngest of four. My sister Roselyn and my twin brothers, Felix and Fowler, had all gone to college. I felt that I wanted to follow their example so, tearfully, I left Miss D to continue school. Whenever the company passed through the Bay Area I took classes and enjoyed being with my friends again.

Miss D continued to be generous of her time with me. An example of this generosity occurred during one of her many returns to the Bay Area while the company appeared at the Mark Hopkins Hotel in San Francisco. I called and asked Miss D if I could bring my students from the Oakland Recreation Department's Division of Modern Dance (of which I was both founder and director) to dance for her. She said she would be happy to see them. I started the girls' "educational process" immediately. First I had to make them aware of the opportunity they would be receiving; second, I had to convince their parents that exposure was an asset to any young dancer's life. With parental approval slips in hand, bag lunches, train fare, and the blessings of the department, we set out for San Francisco.

We were received in the main room of the Mark Hopkins Hotel, The Peacock Court, a large, elegant supper club with white table-clothed tables assembled around a large, square, wooden dance floor. The girls left to get into their costumes of white circular skirts and black leotards while I set up the record player.

Thus, twelve young ladies had the opportunity to meet Miss Dunham and dance for her company. They were also able to meet the writer Langston Hughes, who was visiting at the time, so he was an added bonus. Miss D said that she was happy to see me doing so well in my teaching career.

In 1954 Miss D provided me with yet another big first in my life with the invitation to teach in New York at her Forty-third Street school. Since I had never been to New York, the opportunity to teach in her school seemed too good to pass up. Hurriedly, I obtained a leave of absence from my job and headed nervously for the plane. Fortunately I could stay in the home of my brother Felix, who had married and moved with his family to Westchester County.

For a dancer born and raised in Oakland, going to New York to study was a rare opportunity. But to be on a staff that included people like Geoffrey Holder, Arthur Mitchell, and Louis Johnson was an even greater challenge which allowed me, through daily classes, to expand my dance education.

When the Dunham school unexpectedly closed two months after my arrival due to management difficulties, I returned to Oakland with new inspiration. Immediately I opened my studio of African Haitian dance, which became the first in Oakland to teach Dunham technique.

Miss D had told me so many interesting stories about her research that I was inspired to start my own intensive study. I read everything I could find on African and Caribbean dance and life-styles and never missed a film or travelogue that showed even one dance step.

Soon after the opening of my school I formed a company and

began to choreograph. The Dunham troupe became my basic model. In my work I utilized all I had absorbed while watching Miss D and her production staff. Like a veritable sponge I soaked up interesting lighting methods, costuming techniques, and management procedures, as well as a methodology of concert theater. To this I added my own creative skills. Due to her inspiration I had a highly successful company.

Miss D's awareness of my eagerness for knowledge about dance research techniques would allow me yet another unforgettable opportunity. In 1957 she presented me with the opportunity to manage her estate in Haiti, Habitation Leclerc, formerly the residence of Pauline Bonaparte Leclerc, the sister of Napoleon. I was eager to go. Not only did it mean my first chance to travel to Haiti, but it also provided the opportunity to do field research on the island that, due to my association with Dunham, interested me most.

Yet after much reflection I rejected her offer. I knew that I had no experience in running a large plantation, and I did not want to do a job that would not do justice to the position. On my first trip to Haiti and Habitation Leclerc in 1958, I knew my decision had been correct. Her husband, John Pratt, took me on a tour of the most beautiful land I had ever seen. The estate was huge and quite primitive then; now it is even more enchanting and one of Haiti's main tourist attractions. The best ceremonial dancing, singing, and drumming still occurs nightly at Residence Katherine Dunham and is a treat to both tourists and scholars.

Today I have even greater respect for Miss D's creative genius than I did as her student, as it nurtures her art, but more importantly, as it influences her political beliefs. In the late thirties, a period when it wasn't "in" to do so, she spoke out for racial equality. Today, when I think of her courage in upholding her personal convictions on race, I am inspired.

On the occasions when she has reprimanded would-be segregated audiences (such as in the early forties when she battled the State Department over financial and moral support for her company) or in her present work with the street gangs and police in the East St. Louis slums, she has demonstrated great courage. Furthermore, the stance she took in Europe with English theater managements in the fifties, demanding that African students be allowed to attend performances as her guests involved great risk since it meant a loss of revenue both for herself and for her company.

Her artistic influence on dance is permanent. The Dunham technique is used not only in African and Caribbean dance forms, but also in Afro-American or black dance. Regardless of their race, the effects of her "dance isolation" on students in the black dance style of movement can readily be seen. Even classical ballet corps members have used this style to expand their range of movement.

During one of my trips to East St. Louis to be a guest teacher for Miss D, I was given permission to document her technique on videotape. I felt that this should be done for historical purposes.

All weekly classes she teaches are now videotaped, a procedure that indirectly came about as a result of a conversation I overheard between Miss D and a young woman who was to dance the reconstructed *Floyd's Guitar Blues*. Miss D explained what the dance meant and how the young woman should feel when she performed it. She explained it so beautifully that I said other dancers should have the opportunity to watch her reconstruct her works as well as see and hear her teach master classes.

I began by dividing her technique into "movement periods." Tommy Gomez and I demonstrated the "fundamental period," which I think of as the "theme" of her technique. Lenwood Morris and a student demonstrated the "lyrical period," which smooths, flows, and softens the line of the fundamental. Clifford Fears and the late Ural Wilson demonstrated the "karate A and B periods." As the name implies, Miss D was inspired to create this variation during her stay in Japan in 1958. Karate A and B are very angular and sharp. Fortunately, other instructors at her Performing Arts Training Center (PATC) covered Dunham technique from a time span that encompasses 1938 to the present; thus, as a result of my intervention, PATC has video records of her continued growth and change as an artist.

Whenever I visit her home in East St. Louis, the high point is always the evening meal. Miss D says that, being a true Cancerian, she loves to cook. She insists on preparing meals from scratch rather than using prepared foods. Upon arrival at her home on Tenth Street after a class or meeting, she first prepares a drink of our choice.

Cream of Watercress Soup

(serves eight)

Flour is the deadly enemy in cream sauces. Heavy cream is healthier and tastes better. This is a real cream soup.

about 1-1/2 pounds watercress
3/4–1 cup heavy cream
1 10-3/4-oz. can chicken or beef broth
2 cubes chicken or beef bouillon
pinch of ground nutmeg
salt to taste

Divide the watercress into two bunches, using a fair amount of stem, reserving several sprigs for garnish. Chop coarsely. Simmer half the watercress in a small amount of salted water. When it reduces to a broth, remove it from the stove to cool. Puree the remaining watercress to make about 1 scant cup puree. Next, puree the cooked watercress together with the cream, and add it to the uncooked puree. Add to this mixture the chicken or beef broth along with the two bouillon cubes dissolved in 1 cup of water. Season with a pinch of nutmeg and salt to taste, remembering that the bouillon is salty. Chill. Serve in chilled soup bowls with a sprig of watercress to garnish.

Shrimp Residence (with garlic and coconut)

(serves one as a main course)

[If used as an hors d'oeuvre, the main course should be light, for instance, boned chicken planché on butter (chicken lightly pressed with hands and placed in a skillet), Haitian baked fillet of beef, or red snapper in white wine sauce. As an hors d'oeuvre, the number of shrimp should be halved, and the rice mound made in a small bowl about three inches in diameter or the size of a small ice cream scooper.]

12 jumbo shrimp, peeled and deveined
1 medium clove garlic, minced
grated fresh coconut
2 tbs. butter
2 tbs. peanut oil
rice
raisins
soy sauce (optional)

Clean the shrimp and dry them between paper or cotton towels, flattening each piece into a butterfly shape. Sprinkle the minced garlic on the shrimp. With chopsticks or cooking tongs, dip each side of each piece of shrimp in the coconut, pressing so that the b butterfly shape is maintained. Heat the butter and oil in a skillet. Sauté the shrimp carefully on each side until golden brown. Serve the shrimp arranged in a circle around the edge of a mound of rice dotted with raisins which has been molded in a Chinese rice bowl and turned out onto a serving plate. A sake cup full of soy sauce can be poured over the shrimp and rice if desired. If your guests do not use chopsticks, a fish service is suggested.

My favorite, Haitian rum punch, made in a blender from a recipe whose formula is always kept secret, is a work of art. We relax and talk, and then she starts to prepare the feast. It may be a dish that she started to prepare earlier in the day and let the housekeeper finish, or it may be one she has prepared entirely herself. In either case her cooking is a joy to watch, and even better to eat. I have shared many of her recipes with family and friends after returning home to California. Two are included in this book.

Today she still feels guilty over once having chosen dance as a career in lieu of anthropology, a field in which many helped her to receive grants and an education. She has never stopped justifying their faith in her, often to the degree of pushing herself to the limit of fatigue. Frequently, during the height of performance schedules, she will accept lecture engagements or obligate herself to write papers in order to continue in the scholarly tradition she feels is expected of her. After many years, she realized that her tenure of study in anthropology was not wasted, but had been used uniquely to enhance her dance performances.

On April 5, 1974 I received an important letter: Miss D asked me to write her life's story. Since she did not think she would write a sequel to *A Touch of Innocence* (Harcourt Brace, New York, 1959), in which she described her experiences as a black girl growing up in and around Chicago, she wanted assurance that the rest of her life would be accurately documented by a friend and Dunham dancer.

My first reaction was an emphatic *no*. I was a dancer, not a writer. I felt her life story should be written by some famous "literary" person who could do it justice. After the initial shock wore off, I understood the degree of her trust in our friendship. My pride began to swell to the bursting point as I thought, "Of all the people she could have asked, she has chosen *me*." I had never written a book, but I knew my subject and also knew that over the years a relationship had developed which was based on a fond feeling for each other. Furthermore, I would be a black dancer writing about a black dancer. Once again, she had presented me with a "first."

Writing this book has been one of the greatest challenges in my life. Every word has been written with respect, honor, and great love for my heroine, Miss D.

Childhood
and Undergraduate Days

Glen Ellyn, Illinois. On June 22, 1912, Fanny June and Albert
Millard Dunham brought home from the Chicago hospital their
second child, Katherine. Their only other child, Albert Jr., had been
born six years earlier. Glen Ellyn was a typical white, middle-class
suburb, where the only blacks to be seen wore the crisp white
uniforms of maids or the clean, faded overalls of gardeners and
handymen. At 7:00 in the morning the blacks arrived on public
transportation or caught rides from fellow workers. However, at
7:00 in the evening the bittersweet scene was rewound, like the
strange backstep of a turned-back reel as they left, not daring to
look back at Glen Ellyn.

Fanny June, due to her white skin darkened by American
Indian blood and French–Canadian background, could pass for white
and, as a result, caused enough uncertainty among the white upper
class of Glen Ellyn to be able to purchase land. Albert was thought
to be her chauffeur or handyman, although he was never addressed in
this manner. When Albert saw the land, which lay to one side of a
dirt road newly constructed through a wheatfield, fresh wet cement
sidewalks were still drying. After many meetings of give and take
with developers, coupled with advice and moral support from his
wife, he bought the land. At this time, the city fathers didn't realize
they would be integrating their fine neighborhood. Although Albert
noticed that most new bungalow-type houses were constructed of

brick, shortly after the purchase he laid the foundation for a two-story wooden-frame house.

Once the community discovered that the so-called handyman was really Fanny June's husband, an ad-hoc committee was appointed to plan their eviction. The committee waited for one single building code to be violated; then, after working long into the night, going over and over the building code laws, they found a rule to enforce. They decided Albert's wooden-frame house was in the brick house zone. The wheatfield owner, who would stand to lose, took the new zoning regulation as a personal affront. He opposed the committee and won. Nevertheless, the fever of the committee-men was high and tension grew.

As the truth spread from block to block, so did racial fear and hatred. The explosive situation finally erupted when a bomb shattered every downstairs window Albert had installed. He fought back in the only way he knew—by show of force. A loaded double-barreled shotgun lay across his knees as every night he sat in the front toolshed, a silent, determined guard, ever ready. Then the trouble ceased.

Katherine and Albert Jr. had lived in Glen Ellyn only four years when their mother died of a lingering illness. Fanny June had known for some time that her illness was malignant; she had felt helpless and, as a result, hadn't prepared Albert Sr. for the burden of raising a son and a daughter. Since her older children by a first marriage were burdened by their own problems and children, the only one left to care for Katherine and Albert Jr. was her husband's sister, Lulu. Although Lulu was fond of the children and they of her, her life-style was different from Fanny June's. Whereas the children had been raised in the suburbs, Lulu's ghetto tenement represented an urban situation of the worst kind. Also, among members of Fanny's light-skinned side of the family an inbred snobbism existed toward Albert's more dark-skinned relatives.

As her physical appearance worsened due to her illness, Fanny June absented herself more and more from the children. This con-fused Katherine. Being told to stay away from her mother's room only bewildered her more, and she wondered, "Why do people speak in hushed tones?" and "What is going on behind the closed door?" She felt left out. After an illness of three years, Fanny June died.

After his wife's funeral, Albert Sr. felt completely empty. In his eyes, their seven-year marriage had been perfect. Even during her prolonged illness, Albert had idolized Fanny June, who was twenty years his senior, a divorcee, a mother of five, and grandmother of four. She was an assistant principal in Chicago who had property holdings, whereas he was only a dark-skinned nonestablished tailor, forever humble and grateful.

Following her death, Albert immediately learned that his holdings had been usurped by her older children. Other monies had gone to the hospital and funeral bills of her mother, Grandmother Buckner, and to mentally handicapped Henry, her brother. Thus, after the grief of losing Fanny began to ebb, bitterness moved in. Albert began to hate the light, bright, and "darn-near white" side of the family—it was almost as though sides were drawn up for a battle, the "darks" against the "lights."

After the house was auctioned to pay bills, Albert gave his share of the tailor shop to his partner, George Weir, and took to the road as a traveling salesman. His sister Lulu came and took the children to live with her in Chicago, causing the clean, tree-lined street of Glen Ellyn to give way to the dirty, soot-covered brownstones of a black ghetto. Lulu was a small, dark-skinned, neat woman who accepted Albert's children with love. Although she had always wanted children, she had remained single and childless. For her niece and nephew, living with Aunt Lulu was like being born again in a new land.

Katherine was more than happy to live with Aunt Lulu because she was a beautician who could dress Katherine's crinkled hair which hadn't been combed to the scalp in weeks. Just to know that each braid was parted, oiled, and brushed made a new person of Katherine.

Sometimes Albert would send his sister and children postcards of strange cities and towns he passed through or a money order so small it was spent before it was cashed. Often Aunt Lulu wondered, "Why doesn't Brother let me know where he is? Why doesn't he send more money to help?" Selling men's suits on the road was not lucrative, but Albert Sr. stuck with it. What else could he do?

"How am I going to manage, Lord?" Aunt Lulu's eyes swept the perimeter of the elongated square room in the ghetto of Southside Chicago.

The two chairs of the small apartment were never free of clothes, which gave the room, though it was clean, a somewhat untidy look. With one dresser always overflowing with clothes to "grow into," Katherine's love of wearing "new" clothes was always short-lived. Long before her clothes were ready for disposal they were passed on to other girls in the family, and she would be given the rompers and overalls her brother had outgrown. Then she would be given the hand-me-downs of her half-niece and half-sister, and finally the new, too-long and too-wide clothes of cousins to grow into. She resented this intensely, and wondered if she would ever wear brand-new, "fit-me-now" clothes. But to the four-year-old, clothes as a priority for happiness continued to rotate with other small pleasures in life.

Aunt Lulu, one of the few black hairdressers to work the north side of town, rented a space on the fourth floor of the Fair Building in midtown Chicago, the Loop. For Katherine, Aunt Lulu's world was a key to another way of life. Sometimes Katherine played a game with herself by closing her eyes during the elevator ride to the top of the Fair Building, pretending that the thick, soft carpets of the exclusive beauty salon were heavenly clouds. Everything—the screens, curtains, and lounge chairs—were clean and white and contrasted with the single room she knew too well on the other side of town. Early in the day when business was slow, Aunt Lulu let Katherine sniff the sweet-smelling jars and willingly answered her niece's steady flow of childish "whys," building up Katherine's confidence with each response. A closeness soon grew between them.

Katherine's first problem with racial discrimination concerned the carry-out privileges of the cafeteria in the basement of the Fair Building, where all employees had their meals. The food was the usual cafeteria-style daily menu: stew on Monday; meat loaf with tomato gravy on Tuesday; hot dogs and sauerkraut on Wednesday; a nameless and colorless stewed chicken dish with tasteless dumplings on Thursday; and a fish concoction on Friday. Lulu always took their lunch on a tray to her shop and returned the used dishes before buying the next day's meal. She was frequently greeted with smiles and extra portions that had been set aside for the friendly black woman. So, when an embarrassed clerk informed her she could no longer have this convenience, Lulu's protest was emphatic.

The next indication of the Fair Building problem occurred when Lulu suddenly found that her lease was nonrenewable. Her tears and reminders of verbal agreements made over the years did no good. Even the appeal of influential patrons was of no avail. She had lived in her own little world and couldn't believe this was happening. She had seen the sudden influx of southern Negroes, but since she was a native, not a newcomer, had felt secure. Since the black newcomers posed a severe threat to the job market, poor and middle-class whites believed that refusing jobs to blacks in all areas of society was their only weapon. The lesson of "sameness" seemed to hit with a sickening thud: She was experiencing racial discrimination.

"What can I do with my customers?" Aunt Lulu wondered. "Lord knows they won't come to the South Side. Maybe they would like home service? I could fix a little tote case, and they could get the same service in the convenience of their homes." Her worries were endless. Fortunately, her customers remained faithful and loyal, so money kept dribbling in.

By now Albert Jr. was in elementary school, so Lulu's next concern was to decide what to do with her niece during the day. Katherine was still too young for school and not old enough to be left alone, so a "musical chairs" of babysitters started. Katherine was shifted from neighbor to neighbor. Some homes pleased her and some didn't. The sensitive child could almost instinctively feel a warm or cold atmosphere as she stepped on the threshold of each dingy apartment. Aunt Lulu soon realized that this was not a satisfactory arrangement. Since she felt better leaving Katherine with "family," the only thing left to do was to move in with other relatives.

And what relatives! Uncle Arthur, a vocal coach and choral director, was of medium build and had a quick and easy smile. He took great pride in the timbre of his voice, and spoke constantly. Aunt Clara and her daughter Irene were also singers. Aunt Clara was a robust woman with skin the color of old, darkened copper, although a reddish tone could still be seen. Irene was a carbon copy of her mother. From their weight it was evident that they both loved food. The move into the "family" home resulted in Katherine's first experience with black "show biz," a transfusion that would continue to flow in her veins and would later sustain the world of the dancer Katherine Dunham.

Uncle Arthur was director of the show *Minnehaha* that rehearsed every day in the basement. Quietly sitting on the cellar stairs, Katherine secretly imagined herself in each of the roles. Aunt Clara tilted her head back, opened her mouth wide, closed her eyes, and sang. Such a voice! Katherine never forgot it. The performers danced an elaborate foot-stomping movement in a circle and wore war paint and Indian costumes that completely entranced her. Since everybody had such a good time in this make-believe world, Katherine began to dream of a life in the theater.

Since their mother's death, Katherine and Albert Jr. had become allies. He was more than just her big brother; he was her protector, teacher, and friend. She thought he knew everything. He read every book he could from school and the public library and was always at the head of his class. Every day she waited anxiously for him to return from school so they could exchange daily experiences. She would show him dance steps she had seen rehearsed that day, or those she had created herself. He read stories to her and later taught her how to read and do arithmetic.

When Katherine was barely five, Aunt Lulu summoned Albert Jr. and Katherine and told them she'd received a letter from their father. He had married a lady named Annette Poindexter. The children were suspicious, and wondered what she would look and be like.

"You'll be a family again," Aunt Lulu said. "You'll have a new mother."

"I'll never have a new mother! I'll never have a new mother!" the children echoed each other.

"You'll have a new mother and you'll show them that I brought you all up right and proper, too. You'll live in Joliet, Illinois and you'll be a family."

Aunt Lulu had raised them to be courteous. Therefore, they decided to be polite to the new Mrs. Dunham, but never to call her "mother." Besides, where was Joliet? Katherine wondered if she would still get to attend rehearsals and watch people sing and dance. Albert Jr. thought to himself, "Why did Papa have to go and get married anyway?" They were happy with Aunt Lulu and the family. Katherine didn't want to leave her new-found fascination with the theater; Albert didn't want to leave his school and chums. These troubled thoughts kept tumbling through their heads.

Annette, the new Mrs. Dunham, surprised them. She was kind and gentle, and took great pleasure in cooking their favorite dishes. Their house was never out of order. Best of all, she made Katherine new dresses that she didn't have to grow into—not only dresses, but dresses with matching ruffled petticoats. Katherine and Albert Jr.'s defenses slowly melted away and were replaced with love and trust for their new mother.

Meanwhile, Albert Sr. had tired of being a traveling salesman and decided to try his hand at another aspect of the clothing business. He opened a dry cleaning store, the West Side Cleaners, on Bluff Street in Joliet. The store was located in the smaller half of a building that also housed a rug cleaning business. An elderly man, Mr. Crandall, leased the entire two stories. Although Albert would eventually will him into retirement and one day lease the entire establishment himself, that day was far from being reality. So the couple set out to make their portion as attractive as possible for business. Fortunately, Annette was an accomplished seamstress and sewed curtains for the windows and showcases of the shop, adding light and color. Her job was to do mending and alterations for customers. Not many shops offered this service.

The Dunham family lived in the two-story shop. The parents slept on a double cot in the front room between the counter and hanging clothes; the children slept in the back room on a daybed and cot that were sandwiched between the pressing machine and worktables. Each night the hour for retirement depended on the time the last customer vacated the premises. Then the beds could be set up.

After several years, Mr. Crandall relinquished the building to Dunham, allowing his family to make their home in the upstairs apartment. Furniture was taken out of storage, scrubbed, and shined, and the apartment was converted into a cozy home. Although not at the pace he originally had hoped for, Albert Sr.'s cleaning business grew and expanded.

Deep in the pit of his stomach, Albert Sr. began to fester resentment toward his son. Whereas some fathers would have been proud of a son's scholarly traits, Albert Sr. felt angry. He wanted his son to be learning the cleaning business instead of wasting time on books and talk about college. As a result of this resentment, the father began to nag and pick on the boy if he burned too much fuel at night with the store study lamp or if he seemed preoccupied with thoughts of his own that did not involve the cleaning business.

To keep down dissention, Albert Jr. was obedient. In spite of his father's wishes, he was determined to go to college and study philosophy. Yet the discord between the two men continued to grow. Throughout high school and junior college days, Albert Jr. endured his father's wrath. Finally, he was presented with the opportunity to apply for a full tuition scholarship at the University of Chicago. He jumped at the chance, for it meant, if he received it, the opportunity to leave home.

He had saved what little money he could from meager wages he earned at the shop. Since the scholarship he received was for tuition only, he knew it would not be adequate. When he asked Albert Sr. for an allowance until he could find work in Chicago, his father responded by striking him. His father's action stunned not only Albert Jr., but also his mother and sister. The boy said nothing—he was used to his father's display of anger—it simply made him even more determined to leave.

As Albert Sr. became tense and disillusioned with the cleaning business, the brunt of his frustration focused more and more on his wife and children. First his insecurity amounted to a short angry word here and there; then it was projected through displays of physical violence. The crack and snap of the leather belt became a sound frequently heard in the home. Next Albert Sr. became possessive of all of his family's free time. If Annette was sewing for Katherine or Albert Jr. was studying, he became angry and would shout, "Come help me in the shop." His constant fits of anger soon built up a wall of fear between his children and himself. When Annette tried to protect them from his wrath, he became even more disagreeable.

The frequent quarrels of her father and mother frightened

Katherine. Their shouts and accusations became a way of life around the shop; the house was rarely quiet. Time and time again Katherine heard her father shout to Annette, "If you don't like it here, why don't you leave?"

Katherine always prayed that her mother wouldn't leave because she couldn't bear to live alone with her father. Yet one day the inevitable did happen. Although her parents' previous conflicts had always been verbal, a violent physical struggle took place and, when Katherine returned from school, the shop was empty. What she knew and feared had happened: Annette had left her father. Trying to put the realization of her plight out of her mind, Katherine kept busy and did small chores: She washed dishes, cleaned drawers, rearranged her clothes closet, and cooked. Nevertheless, she felt sad and betrayed.

When her brother returned to the shop she became hysterical. Katherine knew he was soon due to leave for the university, and she was afraid of being alone with her father. Albert Jr. tried to soothe her fears by telling her they would hear from Annette and that she would return. When he realized that he was getting nowhere he said, "Kitty (his pet name for her), wouldn't you like to go to the university, too, after junior college?"

"Yes, but it would cost a lot of money, and I'd never get a scholarship like you did," she answered.

"Don't you worry—by that time I'll be able to help you. Just keep going and ignore Papa and his rantings. One day we'll be together at the university. Don't give up—you'll make it."

Katherine gained strength from her brother's words. The weeks that followed Annette's departure were trying. Her father became sullen and preoccupied. The chores were too many for the hours of the day. She had to stop after-school dance classes to hurry home and label clothes or keep books. For days, no word arrived from her stepmother. "Where can she be?" Katherine wondered.

Finally, a small, blue envelope addressed to the children in Annette's familiar, even handwriting arrived. Eagerly they opened the letter, but it contained no news of a return. Their stepmother had only written to explain why she couldn't stay with their father any longer and to say that they should continue to be good children.

Reading the letter, her brother again said that Annette would be back, although Katherine still thought otherwise. She was proven wrong when another letter came announcing the arrival of Annette's train. Katherine was beside herself with joy. Every hour at school that day seemed to drag. Finally, she was running home to greet her mother. Spontaneously, she ran into waiting arms. The show of physical affection between them was at first both foreign and embarrassing. After they realized what had happened, their bodies slowly separated from their intense embrace. A new warmth grew between mother and daughter. Sadly, the troubled routine of the shop returned as though there had been no interruption. Her father continued to have uncontrollable outbursts of rage.

The one luxury Albert Jr. allowed himself from the meager wages he earned from his work at the shop were cello lessons. Once again, Albert Sr. expressed resentment toward his son, feeling that the time Albert Jr. spent practicing the cello lessened the time he would spend on his chores. Nevertheless, since the boy never started to practice until his night delivery duties were completed, his father couldn't complain. Each week Albert Jr. asked his father for his salary and would then use a portion of the money to pay for lessons. One week Albert Sr. refused to pay him, which caused a heated argument between the two men. Contrary to his usual complacent response, Albert Jr. fought back. Suddenly the house was transformed into four walls of hysteria. Annette screamed; Katherine stood petrified, unable to move. Finally a neighbor came to separate the men as Albert Jr. hissed at his father, "I'll kill you!"

The words momentarily froze his father's fury. He had never had this reaction from his son before, and instinctively felt that his threat was not an idle one. He shouted to his son, "Get out of my house, and never come back."

Stoically, like a determined robot, Albert Jr. packed his meager belongings in a box and left home. He was not heard from again until he wrote asking for help until he could find a job. When Albert Sr. refused his own son's plea for food money, Annette could stand it no longer. After pleading with her husband to come to their son's aid, she was answered with a powerful slap across her face. She had reached the end of her endurance once again. She told Katherine to pack her things and come with her to a house she had rented from her friend, Rebecca Brown. For the first time since Annette's return, mother and daughter happily talked for hours on end without fear of being disturbed by Albert Sr. A temporary calm settled in their new home.

Albert Sr. then offered Annette a job sewing for his shop, but in her own home. Since she needed the money, Annette reluctantly accepted her husband's offer. Katherine also agreed to work in the West Side Cleaners after school. Except for the few hours spent working for the shop, Annette and Katherine were content. In spite of their happiness, they missed Albert Jr.

Katherine was a dual person during her days at the Beale Grammar School. She was a leader and very aggressive in sports, but shy in social relationships. She thought of a way to combat her fear of people by forming her own club and becoming its president. Since the days when she watched *Minnehaha* in rehearsal, she had been fascinated by American Indians. Consequently, the elementary school club she established was named the "Eagle Eye." It was a small secret club with only a few members Katherine selected herself. She begged her mother for scraps of materials and beads from the shop so that each girl could bead her own single eye in the middle of an Indian-type band worn on the forehead. Every day after school, members would decide on a project to explore or sit at least half an hour beading their Eagle Eye bands. When Katherine's teachers and principal heard about her secret organization, she was told to disband it. Nevertheless, club leadership had caused her social ego to meet her expectations.

The Terpsichorean Club, a high school dance organization, met three or four times a week. To belong, one had to pass an audition and, since Katherine was dance-oriented, she easily passed and became a member. The club performed a type of free-style modern dance patterned after Jaques-Dalcroze and Rudolf von Laban.

Jaques-Dalcroze was the originator of Eurythmics in the early twentieth century. His style encompassed a complex rhythmic structure that required the dancer to move just after the beat. He was also one of the pioneers of improvisational movement. Rudolf von Laban was an early pioneer of the modern dance movement and was responsible for Labanotation, a coding used to record dance movement. The gym teacher had only been exposed to these two movement forms.

Katherine's family allowed her to join because club activities seemed harmless and didn't involve boys. Rehearsals were sandwiched between basketball practice and work in her father's shop.

School athletics also proved to be one of Katherine's joys and accomplishments. In the Girls' Athletic Association she excelled in track and basketball and was elected captain of both teams. Furthermore, her innate dancing skills enhanced her timing and coordination in sports.

After a short while, Katherine discovered the beginnings of a knee problem that would be aggravated by further involvement in sports. As a result, she decided to abandon athletics to concentrate solely on dancing. In dance her knees did not hurt as much.

Due to the Terpsichorean Club, she had a good background in free-style movement, but secretly envied girls who had studied ballet. She admired the graceful movement of the arms, or port de bras, and the beautiful tutus, or full, stiff-net skirts. She was fascinated by the strange hard-toed shoes they wore to dance on the tips of their toes, en pointe.

Her father complained, "If you have time to prance around, you'd better spend it doing something useful in the shop." He soon put a stop to after-school games and practices by announcing a stated time to be at the shop that did not allow her time to play or even to stop and talk to her few friends. Still, Katherine continued to practice as much as she could, never forgetting her dance teacher's belief that she had talent and could one day profit from study with teachers in New York.

All through school, Katherine maintained good grades. Latin and French were interesting, science and arithmetic were troublesome, and English literature was one of her favorite courses. Her curiosity about people grew. She thought of neighbors remembered vaguely in Glen Ellyn, the people of South Side Chicago, of Joliet, of Alton (where some of Annette's relatives lived), and of St. Louis. She wondered why people reacted in such different ways to the same situations. In high school no course explained or answered her questions, but Albert Jr. assured her that such a course, called "anthropology," the science of man, existed in college, and that she should study it. Katherine wondered how she would ever get to college and, once there, how would she live and support herself. Her brother promised to help, and Katherine became more determined than ever to graduate from high school with the necessary grades for college.

Her main high school crush was William Booker. Although Bill was a tall, handsome football hero and the idol of all the girls, he was very taken with Katherine. He wasn't concerned that she wore old-fashioned clothes and didn't have the "line" of conversation of other girls. Although Katherine shyly imagined that no one thought her attractive, he thought she was beautiful. One day he asked her to wear his block letter. To Katherine, this was heaven on earth. Only girls who dated got to wear letters, and she wasn't allowed to date, so the impossible seemed to be happening. She took great pains to decide what sweater to sew it on. At least an hour was spent sewing, making certain each stitch was straight and even. Albert Sr., however, had seen Bill and his daughter talking on the bridge several times after school and succeeded in breaking up their company whenever possible by driving by and ordering Katherine into the delivery truck. Luckily Bill was understanding and willing to live for the few precious moments he and Katherine were able to have together. Yet Albert Sr. soon demanded that she return the block letter and placed even more demands on Katherine's time, making it almost impossible for them to be together. In addition to causing her embarrassment in returning Bill's emblem, Albert Sr. accused them of things Katherine didn't really understand and punished her with a severe beating. This was all Katherine could physically and emotionally take from her father. "Touch me again and I'll kill you!" she cried, remembering what her brother had said.

The night following the beating, she lay in bed and felt the welts slowly disappear. Vowing to leave as soon as possible, and for good, she wrote Albert Jr. of her need to get away. When her brother read her letter, he knew he had to figure out a way to free his sister. Not only was he concerned about her unhappiness with their father, but he also felt her talent needed a greater outlet and other cultural stimuli.

Albert Jr. sent her an application for a civil service job in the Hamilton Park Branch Library as a junior library assistant. Since Katherine loved books, it was a natural for her to pass the exam. After convincing her mother that she would be able to support herself when the library job ended, even if it meant washing dishes for a living, Katherine obtained permission to leave. Her brother promised to keep an eye on her.

The library was located in an exclusive part of the city, whose residents had very racist philosophies. It was run by two unmarried sisters, the McLaughlins, who had devoted their entire lives to books. Their world was the white, safe, middle-class suburban community whose only exposure to blacks was one of employer to employee in a domestic situation. So when brown-skinned Katherine appeared at the desk as the employee who had passed the civil service examination with such a high score, the sisters were understandably shocked. Only upper-bracket civil service examination scorers were allowed to work at the Hamilton Library. Immediately the eldest and most aggressive sister started planning what to do with Katherine. Although her classification clearly stated that she would be working with the public, this rule was ignored; she was placed in the back stacks to work, out of public view. This was her most acute personal experience with discrimination.

Although she was hired only for summer employment, the job would eventually provide a way to get away from her father. Odd jobs were hard to get, but Katherine was persistent and somehow she was able, by living very modestly, to support herself.

By the time she entered the University of Chicago, Katherine had decided that she *had* to dance. Knowing she could get advanced training in Chicago more easily than in Joliet, she went after it immediately. Thus, while working in the library and starting her studies in anthropology, she was simultaneously very involved in dance.

She learned through friends that a group of artists needed dancers as models. At the artists' studio, she assured them she could pose in authentic Spanish gypsy dance positions and was offered the job. But while posing, she realized she couldn't hold the slightly bent knee position. Again she was aware of a pain in both knees that had been chronic since childhood. But she badly needed work so she suffered silently. The job, though, made her aware that this was no minor ailment. Consulting a physician, she was told she had chronic arthritis. Katherine told him, "This can't be—I have to dance!"

"If you can stand pain, you can dance; otherwise you must stop," he answered. "There is no cure for your knees."

Hearing this shocking news she decided, "I might just become a famous anthropologist after all. A scholar doesn't have to have strong knees, and that is what I'm studying to be." But another voice in her head said, "I must dance—I love dancing."

She decided to continue to dance, hoping that a cure would be found before her knees became too bad. Sadly, the knee problem would plague her entire career.*

Katherine's days at the University of Chicago were difficult financially. The country was in the Depression and money was at a minimum. In order to stay in school she received student loans and scholarships.† Her brother always tried to help, but he was on a scholarship that gave him a meager assistance with no other finances.

During the first year of school, bad weather added to the normal miseries of undergraduate days. The heat seemed to cook everything in its path; the cold was unbearable. Katherine's mother tried to convince her to wear her old warm high school coat, but her vanity wouldn't let her.

"Mother, I simply can't go to college with my old coat," she said. "I'd rather freeze first." And she did.

When she was seventeen, Annette had made her a party coat from left-over clothes in her father's shop to wear in Chicago while visiting cousins. It was velvet with an old, faded, mink collar and had very little lining. Because she hadn't worn it often, it looked newer than her old "warm coat." Since dresses were short that year,

---

*In Paris in January 1966, surgery would be performed and both knee caps removed. In 1979 Dunham plans to have plastic knee caps surgically implanted.
†In her course of studies, Dunham has received grants from the Rosenwald, Rockefeller, and Guggenheim foundations.

Katherine decided to wear the party coat instead. Pretending not to be cold became her first successful acting role. Because there was no money to pay for heat she couldn't even look forward to cozy, warm evenings at home. Many nights she slept fully clothed for warmth.

Katherine was taking dancing lessons and was the strongest student in her class. A friend suggested that she teach dance privately. She talked it over with her brother and he agreed. But how and where could a suitable and financially feasible location be found? In the bohemian area near the university on Chicago's South Side in a stable they discovered a loft area that would double for living quarters. There she became a full-fledged dance teacher.

Living in the dance studio brought back memories of living in two rooms in the early days of her father's dry cleaning store. Once again she slept on a small cot and was not able to make the studio into a living area until the last student left for the evening. But inconvenience in this situation was welcome. She scheduled her teaching around classes at the university and part-time work in the library, which by now had become permanent. Her teaching helped finance her studies.

At the university she continued to find creative ways to survive, which were invaluable training for the rest of her life. One means of survival allowed her to meet many leading artists of her day. In realizing that his sister needed an outlet for artistic expression, her brother, along with a Greek friend, Nicolas Matsukas, a psychology student, established the Cube Theater Club. In the same block of buildings Katherine met Ruth Page, her first encounter with a choreographer, and Mark Turbyfill, her first ballet teacher. Together they would eventually establish the school that would form the first Negro dance company.

The Cube Theater was located in a set of little wooden buildings that had been built as shops for the 1893 Columbian Exposition. Historically it had been an area used by writers and painters to live and work in and form an art colony. The rent was about twenty dollars a month. Frequently the half-dozen students who composed the Cube Theater would get together and visit different shows as they came through town, entertaining the various artists afterward.

The Cube Theater Club was progressive. Since the artists they

entertained were of both races, members decided that their extra-
curricular activities should be integrated as well. Unfortunately,
black students at the university were reluctant to participate in
these functions. The crowd of the Cube Theater was considered
both offbeat and arty, and for the most part blacks were involved
in their own social life of fraternities and sororities. Some members
of the original theater group who eventually achieved fame included
artists Charles White and Charles Sebree, dramatists Ruth Attaway
and Canada Lee, writer Langston Hughes (when he was in town), a
noted anthropologist, St. Clair Duke, and the musician W.C. Handy.

As Katherine matured, it was her nature to be friendly, but not
chummy. She disliked familiarity. She felt comfortable with fellow
anthropology students and enjoyed parties, but retained few childhood friends. In any area in which she was not familiar, Katherine
Dunham became a willing follower but, when it came to teaching
and slowly forming her unit of dancers, she was a leader with an
eye and a sixth sense about correct movement and clean lines. She
would not accept the dancer who would not respect his or her tool,
the body. At this early time in her career, she had already acquired a
reputation as a strict taskmaster, a disciplined teacher and dancer.
She was never aware that she was a leader. When actively working on
a project, the matter of status never entered her mind.

Some people who watched Katherine's development with
interest were Charles Johnson, a noted sociologist and member of
the Rosenwald Foundation, and Erich Fromm, the psychoanalyst.
Her professors at the university supported her in her thesis on
Dance and Anthropology as a course of study. The premise of this
thesis stated that studying the percussive instruments of ancient
peoples was as valuable as studying their tools in discovering their
living habits. Most tribal groups used some sort of beaters to
accompany dance, drive off evil gods, and attract favorable spirits.
Also, she felt the study of nonverbal comunication or dance was as
important a study as verbal communication or language. Although
she feared that she was stretching a point with her theories, the
university thought her approach was both imaginative and creative.

Katherine's dance classes soon began to present recitals and
shows. These in turn allowed her to experiment with choreography.

The low-key atmosphere and relative lack of pressure from the press and other groups made the climate conducive to experimentation. She was free to create dances and feel an excitement in choreography that would add a new dimension to her career. At the time, no serious black concert dance group existed after which she could pattern her ideas, therefore she had to resort to the white Ballets Russes as a model. Mark Turbyfill and Katherine called the first serious Negro ballet company the Ballet Negre. They spoke with Eric Delamarter, the assistant conductor of the Chicago Symphony and a good friend of Mark's, seeking ideas and help. He convinced them that they should establish a school because every important company had one. Slowly they began to gather students willing to work hard toward the distinction of being the first Negro ballet company.

The company's debut took place at the annual Beaux Arts Ball in 1931. Although they were a great hit at the ball, they were ahead of their time. The public was not ready to support a touring black concert dance group that did not have minstrel show overtones. Katherine's choreography, *Negro Rhapsody*, was well received, but so were the other numbers in the show, and her group was soon forgotten. No engagements followed and, as the troupe slowly disbanded, once again her brother bolstered her confidence. "You just had back luck! Try a new approach," he said. "The idea is great!"

Ludmila Speranzeva, her modern dance teacher, also guided and inspired her to keep on working toward her goal. She suggested that Katherine should teach only modern dance.

Katherine called the next set of dancers the Negro Dance Group. Because she was a perfectionist and her dancers were unwilling to follow strict rehearsal and training schedules, this company also failed. Her depression finally lifted when Ruth Page invited her to dance with the Chicago Civic Opera, where her excellent performance as one of the solo leads was effective in bringing more students to her school. Nevertheless, the turnover was great because Katherine wouldn't lower her standards to pacify lazy students. She continued to choreograph and produce studio performances along with special showings at the Cube Theater and in private homes.

On the evening of one of her shows, Mrs. Alfred Rosenwald

Stern of the Rosenwald Foundation was in the audience. The foundation was one of the few noted for giving financial aid to struggling artists, especially blacks. Katherine was positive that Mrs. Stern was in attendance only because of her good friend Erich Fromm's insistence.

Mrs. Stern was impressed with the performance. Before long, Katherine was asked to appear before the board of the Rosenwald Foundation to present her revolutionary ideas on anthropology and dance.

While waiting for her audience with the board, Katherine experienced many anxious moments. Constantly she asked herself, "Should I present myself as anthropologist first and dancer second, or vice versa? Should I wear my best clothes or look truly in need of financial aid? Should I dance? Should I volunteer information or wait for their questions?"

She finally decided to wear a stylish, old, salt-and-pepper tweed suit, a white tailored blouse, and black, comfortable oxfords over her dance uniform, a black leotard and calf-length black bias-cut skirt. Just in case she was asked to dance she wouldn't keep them waiting while she changed.

Finally, she was in the meeting room with the awesome board members. The chairman started the interview by asking, "What course of study would you pursue if you were given enough funds to explore your thesis?"

After thinking a moment, a slow smile came to her eyes, lighting up her entire face. She knew her course of action. "It's a bit difficult to put into words," she answered. "Do you mind if I show you?"

The staid board members were a little shocked when she unbuttoned her jacket and skirt and stepped out in her dance togs. She then performed stereotyped ballet movements such as arabesques, port de bras, and pirouettes; then added modern dance movements that would be familiar to the board such as floor rolls, contractions, and leaps. She calmly stated, "That is what is being taught in Chicago and in most dancing schools of the country."

Then she caused the room to seemingly vibrate with an African dance that finished by leaving the entire board speechless. Her head, shoulders, rib cage, hips, and legs moved in such a contrasting style to that of her first demonstration; it seemed impossible that both were performed by the same body. Without any percussion accompaniment, her movements created a pulsating feeling that brought to one's imagination the exotic beats of *vaudun*,* or *voodoo*, drums.

After Katherine's impromptu show, the board thanked her. She redressed and left. Because she was afraid to believe that she would get the fellowship, the wait for the board's decision filled her with impatience and concern. She considered herself a good investment, but also realized that she had to be practical. She began to think of alternatives in case she wasn't selected. By now, the Hamilton Branch library staff had become more liberal, so she decided that one alternative would be to advance to the position of senior librarian and continue her education. She could at the same time try to make her studio, which she shared with the black dramatist Ruth Attaway, more profitable with backing from rich blacks who hadn't supported her before. Nevertheless, the thought of staying in Chicago made her depressed; she had already reached her performance peak there and knew it.

Since it provided a black person with talent the best opportunities to choreograph and had the best schools, New York became another choice. Still, since she was at the point in her career where her ideas on choreography and staging were not yet formed, Katherine didn't know if she had the courage to go to New York for further training.

For the first time, she felt uncertain about the future. She knew the Rosenwald Foundation's decision would be a turning point in her life. Not only would it determine the course her career as a dancer would take, but it would also decide the course she would take as historian and anthropologist.

---

* The reader is referred to the glossary for the definition of Haitian, West Indian, and other special terminology.

Caribbean Field Research

Finally, the letter with the return address "The Rosenwald Foundation" arrived. A joy rushed over Katherine like a warm shower. As her nervous fingers hurriedly began to open the envelope, a lingering fear slowed down the process as her worries continued: "Suppose they felt my idea too experimental? Maybe my dance demonstration was too earthy. Maybe I should have talked more."

All her fears were fantasy, because the short, official letter simply stated that she had been awarded a fellowship for her Caribbean research. Katherine was overwhelmed by the news. When the board room had finally settled down after her rousing dance demonstration, they had unanimously approved her grant. So in February 1935 she was given $2400 for preparatory study and one year of research away from home. Of the sum, $500 was earmarked for living expenses and tuition at Northwestern University and the balance, $1900, was for actual research undertaken in the West Indies.

Katherine's naivete in practical matters led her to believe that, once the fellowship was received, she could simply secure a plane reservation and take off, free to explore on her own. She was therefore surprised to find herself enrolled in a nine-month course of preparatory study with Melville Herskovits, head of the Anthropology Department at Northwestern. Dr. Herskovits immediately won her respect by his great knowledge in the field of anthropology.

In his teaching he was very patient, but also demanding. He made it clear to Katherine that her very life might depend on her fully absorbing the lessons he would be teaching her on survival. From Herskovits she learned how to use snake bite kits, what diseases to look for, how to avoid them, and what to do in case of the most common health hazard, water pollution. Also, she learned how to methodically pack personal effects such as soap, toothpaste, sanitary napkins, and canned goods. She was briefed on the use and storage of recording and photographic instruments. Because of the tropical humidity that causes mildew, she was told to pack all her equipment in airtight containers.

Herskovits stressed the importance of not offending people in the West Indies and cautioned her to be aware and sensitive to body language and customs. She was told how to behave. To the young, free-spirited black American who believed in equality of the sexes, the double standard set for West Indian men and women by their society was very strange. In her book *Island Possessed* (Doubleday, Garden City, N.Y., 1969), she writes, "Middle class and upper class Haitians operated, at the time, on hospitality codes more French than American. At home, wives and daughters were seldom in evidence to visitors, remaining inside, from where they peeked through wooden shutters at husbands and sons entertaining on the veranda."

The last area of instruction was a course on how to keep proper research records, since the Rosenwald Foundation would expect thorough reporting on their investment. After returning, she would be expected to present papers on her findings. The mere fact that a black woman would be visiting and investigating other blacks automatically added a new dimension to the research that even an experienced, well-equipped, white anthropologist such as Herskovits could not foresee. Katherine would be able to see the art and the dances of the West Indies and respond to them on the level of a fellow black artist and dancer; in that sense, her observation would be far more valid than those of former researchers. She would in turn benefit by applying the results of her nine months' research to her career as a performer.

Herskovits stressed the importance of printing calling cards with two titles, "Dancer" and "Anthropologist," so she would have an entry into the two fields.

Katherine's send-off was very low key. She borrowed a little red typewriter from Jack Harris, a colleague in Herskovits' class, in order to keep methodical records. After traveling by train to Joliet to say good-bye to family and friends, she took her first plane ride to Washington, D.C. to get her passport and say farewell to her brother, by now a professor at Howard University. Finally she left for her departure point, New York.

Since Herskovits had impressed upon her the importance of her attendance at various social functions for governors, presidents, and the press that would take place during her travels, she embarked on a last-minute shopping spree at Saks Fifth Avenue, where she spent a large portion of her grant on clothes. Among other purchases she bought a dress with a little train which she wore only once to a garden party.

Nevertheless, to a woman with her background of hand-me-downs, the temptation to buy new things without restrictions was irresistible. She would later find out that, once deeply involved in her work, she wouldn't need them. She would spend as much time as possible in work clothes. An old corduroy skirt or riding breeches, a shirt, heavy stockings, and oxfords or boots would become her uniform.

When she embarked on her first sea voyage, only a few friends were at the dock. She was excited and anxious to go to sea. Just boarding the small ship owned by the Royal Netherlands Company was an experience. She pinched herself to realize that the trip was finally underway. A young, lone black woman from Illinois, poor but ambitious, she was on her way to the exotic West Indies on an assignment previously unheard of in anthropological studies. She would visit Haiti, Jamaica, Martinique, and Trinidad before returning to Haiti for a final, more intensive period of study in dance and anthropology. These islands had been selected because of the continued influence of dance on the lives of their people.

The moment Katherine saw the lush green topography and the turquoise sea, felt the tropical climate, and met the friendly, proud inhabitants, her love affair with the Caribbean islands that had no interlude began.

Arriving on each island, her first job was to secure living quarters and contact people to assist with her field study. The excited traveler stayed six weeks with the Maroon people in Accompong, Jamaica, a visit that later resulted in her book *Journey to Accompong* (Henry Holt and Co., New York, 1946). Her fascination with the Maroons centered itself on their ability to stay free of Spanish and English rule and keep their life-style as close as possible to that of their African ancestors. Their story was known throughout the Caribbean.

When Katherine landed in Jamaica, she boarded a small train and headed for "Maggotty." The train ride took her high into the "Blue Mountains." In Maggotty she was met by her guide, "the Colonel," whom Herskovits had alerted of her arrival. (During a brief stay with the Maroons, Herskovits had found the Colonel to be both informative and respected in the community.) After she presented her letter of introduction, the Colonel drove her to the town of Whitehall. From that point on, transportation was by mule. She had never ridden a mule before and was uncomfortable with the thought of having to do so, but ride she did.

During the first few moments of the mule ride she was frightened and too uncomfortable to do anything but hang on to the slow-moving, hairy bulk. As she began to get the knack of the animal's rhythm and fit her movements to his, she began to relax and let her gaze wander to the landscape around her. The Maroons' main occupation was farming. When the Maroons first arrived in Accompong they were hunters, but as game, mostly wild boar, began to dwindle, they began to work the land. The fertile land provided lush breadfruit, banana, mango, and coffee trees, each with its own fragrance to add to the beautiful aromas of the tropical flowers. The mountains were so steep they seemed to travel straight upward into the sky. She felt compassion for the native luggage bearers, who had to contend with the steep terrain while simultaneously supporting the weight of bulky, heavy bags. Happily, their curiosity about the black American woman who had come to live among them seemed to lighten their load. Upon the party's arrival at the Colonel's two-room hut, a group of Maroons were already following, parade style, and staring openly at Katherine Dunham, the town's new curio. Because

she knew that she was the first black American woman they had
ever seen, and that their interest was genuine, she tried hard to remember patience and empathy. For her first dinner in Accompong she
was fed a delicious meal of breadfruit, peas and rice, and curried lamb.

The weary traveler was to occupy one of the two hut's rooms.
Katherine tried to ignore the curious stares from the rest of the
household. She was very tired so she went to bed as soon as it was
proper to excuse herself, knowing that the present living arrangement
just wouldn't work. She felt she couldn't impose herself in that
fashion on the Colonel's family. After a restful sleep, the following
morning her host announced that he had solved the lodging problem
by finding her a house to rent. She gladly moved farther up the
mountain into a two-room hut and began unpacking. The hut had no
kitchen, so food was prepared in a separate, smaller hut in back,
where it was cooked in kettles over an open fire. Knowing she
wouldn't have time to learn to cook the new, exotic dishes, especially over an open fire, she hired a woman to assist her. Herskovits had
told Dunham that this was also a matter of prestige in the village.

When Katherine was settled, the Colonel began an·oral history
of the Maroon people. Although she was grateful for the fine information, she kept reminding him that dance was what she wanted
most to learn about. One night she was treated to a dance on the
"parade," a large, flat area on the hilltop overlooking the village.
Villagers came from far and near; Jamaican white rum was served in
abundance; people spoke in soft, melodic voices, greeting each other
and choosing partners; and finally they began the dance. Two lines
were formed, men in one and women in the other. In this formation,
they began to dance a version of the European Quadrille to which a
syncopated beat had been added. Though Katherine was disappointed
to see West Indians doing this type of dance, as the evening wore on
and the rum flowed, the local drummers carried the crowd to an
ever-higher pitch where the "set dances" gave way to freer, more
rhythmic, hip-swinging dance forms. Women used mid-calf-length
skirts to strut and spin; men performed acrobatic flips and leaps.

Throughout the West Indies, a woman well into her sixties
could easily become belle of the ball, and age of course gave more
experience in executing steps. Katherine noticed that the most

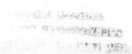

popular women at dances were older women in their sixties and seventies. She also noticed that young people respected their elders and would watch intently from the sidelines. Some practiced the dances of their parents in little groups, out of the limelight, mentally rushing the time along for their chance to be dancers. From this early stage of mimicking, a friendly competition would begin which allowed the best dancers among the young peers to become, in the future, the adult lead dancers.

When Katherine finally felt secure with the steps, she danced the *Shay Shay* with the Colonel, moving her body with complete joy and excitement over the free and sensuous dance movement. When she became exhausted and had to rest, she noticed that women far her senior were fresh and going strong. Their dancing revitalized them. Retiring, she left them dancing until the early dawn.

In Accompong, one of her greatest desires was to see the war dance, *Koromantee*, named after a West African tribe. *Koromantee* is a dance of preparation for war, and contains movements that stimulate aggressive behavior. Women shake rattles and men swing sticks at imaginary enemies. Occasionally a woman grabs a man's shoulders and shakes them, trying to arouse in him even more hostility. The Goombay drum, a square, wooden drum that was played with a beater, is used for rhythm. Later, Katherine decided to have a replica of this drum constructed for her own use.

From Jamaica, Katherine traveled to Haiti which, because it contained the greatest amount of dance, became her favorite Caribbean island. Other islands were more acculturated yet contained fewer African remnants. In contrast, Haiti appeared a proud black republic whose roots were still firmly planted in Africa, the mother-land.

In 1804, Haiti was the second country in the Western Hemisphere to become a republic. Throughout the nineteenth century, the country was torn by civil strife, revolution, and internal disaster. In 1923, the U.S. government decided that Haiti would be a protectorate of the United States. Unfortunately, a group of U.S. Marines from the southern states were given political control of the country which lasted until 1934. A number of bitter battles took place between the marines and the Haitian fighting peasants, called *cacos*.

For the Haitians, the clash with the marines was their first encounter with white racism since before their successful revolution against the colonists.

Haitians were used to a color caste system based on the premise that the lighter the skin, the more white blood mixture. The very light-skinned were mulattos, or elite, and included professional workers, shop owners, bank clerks, and the wealthy. Their air of superiority was passed on from generation to generation. In contrast, the very dark Haitian, or peasant, usually included the poor, menial labor force. If by chance a black Haitian is educated and rich, he is allowed to function as a mulatto, but never socially accepted as an equal.

Because the marines did not differentiate by skin tone, it was of the greatest importance to unify the light-skinned mulattos and the black peasants. To the "fighting Yanks," all Haitians were black, and thus inferior.

Haiti was released from the marine occupation in 1934. Katherine was impressed by the knowledge that every Haitian peasant, whether he lives high in the hills or in the waterfront slums of Port-au-Prince, feels pride in the status of his republic which has earned its independence. They know independence was won by the peasants themselves instead of by the mulattos, or generals. The peasants would thus never allow the island be taken over by a foreign state again. In Haiti, for the first time in her life, Katherine felt part of a majority instead of a minority. There was no discrimination. She felt proud to see blacks in charge of their destiny and running things. Haiti was *their* business.

The value of Herskovits' letters of introduction shifted according to the occasion. Although they were able to facilitate her research, they also aroused a certain amount of suspicion. For instance, she did not deliver the letter given to her for the president of Haiti, Tenio Vincent, until after her year of research had almost ended and she was preparing to leave. She didn't want to become too involved with the Haitian mulatto elite while working with Haitian peasants. Her letters to the governor of Trinidad had also been of purely social value. Her most helpful letters were those addressed to anthropologists and researchers, particularly those letters to a librarian, Carlton Comma, in Trinidad and a newspaper editor in

Jamaica. It was of crucial importance to know how and when to use her letters of introduction; thus she began to depend more and more on her own instincts rather than on those of Herskovits.

During her travels she loved to collect old books and frequently headed for libraries. In Jamaica she found an old volume on the Maroon people that told of their struggle to overcome the British Army, which was similar to the story she later discovered in Haiti. The book documented how the Maroons under Cudjoe, their leader, forced the British Army to give them a plot of land. At that time Accompong was tax-free and autonomous. Another library discovery was a book that had been written by Moreau de Saint-Mery, a researcher and writer, which she used as a text and read during her travels.

In order to thoroughly study Caribbean literature, Katherine had to do an extensive study of both the French and Spanish languages. The only countries of the Caribbean that she visited which were English speaking were Jamaica and Trinidad. Katherine's knowledge of Latin helped her deciper Spanish. Later she would recommend that all students planning to do research in either Africa or the West Indies have a firm foundation in both languages.

Another of Herskovits' letters of introduction was to Dr. Jean Price-Mars, a distinguished anthropologist who had run for the presidency of Haiti on several occasions and thoroughly knew the land, the people, and their religion, the *vaudun*. He guided the young researcher in her travels over the island and interpreted what she saw. Furthermore, Price-Mars had friends who still lived in a folk state very close to that of their African forefathers. His assistance and knowledge thus enabled Katherine to be accepted by many "people of the interior." Other friends who aided her research were René Piquion and Doc Reeser. Doc was a ship's pharmacist and ex-marine who had stayed in Haiti after the occupation simply because he loved the island.

Her first home in Haiti was the Excelsior Hotel, managed by the two Rouzier sisters. Because of their light-yellow skin tone, Katherine knew they were of the elite class. With their wealth of knowledge of their own class customs, they were helpful in exposing her to members of Haiti's social elite.

Due to the frequent visits of Katherine's many unorthodox friends, the Rouziers were kept in a constant state of agitation. One moment she would be entertaining Dr. Lherisson, a mulatto professional of fine family background who was perfectly respectable to the sisters; the next moment she would entertain Price-Mars, an intellectual who had been popular enough to run for president and almost win, yet who nevertheless was black, and hence not acceptable.

Fred Allsop, also a friend of Dunham's, was a white Englishman, yet because he worked as an automobile mechanic, he was not accepted by the Rouzier sisters. Nevertheless, in their narrow opinion, he was a step above the black peasant so frequently he broke the caste barrier of the Rouziers and visited.

Among Katherine's favorite visitors were the peasants she had met in her research with Price-Mars: Téoline, Cécile, and Dégrasse. They would come to the area directly across the street from the Excelsior and, after sending word to the household servants to give her a message they were there, they would wait for her to see them. They never waited long because Katherine would run to where they stood waiting, greeting them with open affection. These peasants were the people she wanted to know, for they were still close to their African heritage. They lived high up in the "green mountains" of Haiti and would bring her news of the *vaudun* ceremonies of births and deaths. Katherine's comings and goings with all colors and classes of people made her situation tolerable but puzzling to the two Rouzier spinsters and to other mulattoes.

She realized on her first trip that many travelers to Haiti were offended by the prevailing poverty. Yet the feeling of pride and the sense of freedom that she related to in the poor people caused her to momentarily forget their discomfort. On one occasion she visited the Iron Market, the true slums of Haiti, with Deputy Dumarsais Estimé, the president of the Chamber of Deputies.

The Iron Market is a place of organized confusion which covers two large blocks in downtown Port-au-Prince. It is famous for its iron archway of a rusty green and red color. The street between the two blocks is a street vendor's paradise because the stalls spill out onto the mall-like shopping area. The noise of honking horns, the vendors chanting their wares, the gossip of hill peasants whose day at the market is a social event, and the voices of children hustling tourists to be their guide shouting "I speak Engleesh, Missy" is heard every-where. (The peasant child, whose native language is *patois*, or Creole French—a language using some African, Spanish, and French words, with a musical sound and rhythmic flow—has also had to learn English. With English he communicates with the tourist and sells his wares and services.)

The odor of the Iron Market is a combination of smells: fresh and decaying fish, live poultry, produce, and sweaty bodies. Beggars with physical afflictions purposely expose a nubbed hand or stump of a leg to point out their need for one's coins. Women on child-sized wooden chairs sit along curbs and sell their limes or mangos piled in pyramid shapes. In another area of the market, old pedal sewing machines produce garments on a Haitian-type assembly line. For the sophisticated tourist, very fine mahogany sculpture pieces or beautiful oil paintings can be purchased, but only after skillful and playful bargaining takes place. Anything from bean necklaces to hand-carved household furniture can be bought. Soon the streets are so crowded that to walk in a straight line is impossible; a weaving motion must be used to make one's way through the crowd.

Katherine was horrified. Nevertheless, because she had exper-ienced severe poverty on Chicago's South Side, she was able to overlook the conditions of poverty such as those she saw in the Iron Market of Port-au-Prince and devote full attention to the hill and plains peasant. The impoverished peasant, living outside the city, still had his own plot of land, his own pride, his own extended family, and most important, his own sense of ownership and freedom.

During this period of field research, Dunham was laying the groundwork for a career of continued research and performance. The investigative techniques she learned were tools that could be used in other countries during her later travels. In the West Indies she developed the sensitivity not only to travel in a strange country, but also to feel at ease and in harmony with its people. Because of the time invested in her Rosenwald grant, touring days with her company were smoother and more enjoyable.

Katherine Dunham's Haitian excursion has been carefully annotated in a small book, probably the first combining the study of dance and anthropology, *The Dances of Haiti*,* written by Dunham and used as a text at the Performing Arts Training Center in East St. Louis, as well as in numerous other U.S, cities and foreign countries. It was first published in Mexico in 1947, and today serves as a guide to many dance and anthropology students.

*Katherine Dunham, *The Dances of Haiti*, Mexico D.F., November 1947.

Katherine in a goat-drawn cart of a traveling photographer (*from the collection of Katherine Dunham*)

Katherine and Albert Jr. (*from the collection of Katherine Dunham*)

Katherine Dunham and John Pratt during their courtship, 1939 (*from the collection of Katherine Dunham*)

Marie Christine, Dunham and Pratt's daughter (*from the collection of Katherine Dunham*)

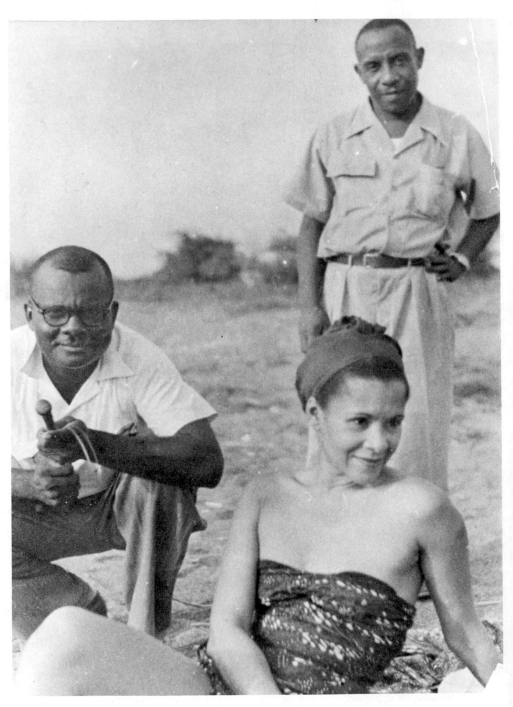

Katherine Dunham with her Haitian friends during her early research (*from the collection of Katherine Dunham*)

Katherine Dunham with President Leopold Senghor of Senegal, Africa, 1962 (*from the collection of Katherine Dunham*)

Katherine Dunham receiving a Distinguished Service Award from Chancellor Rendleman of the University of Chicago, 1969 (*photo by Charles H. Cox*)

Ruth Beckford assisting Katherine Dunham in her role as a visiting professor in the Afro-American Department at the University of California at Berkeley, 1976 (*photo by Francine Jamison*)

Getting the Show
on the Road

"Miss D," as she would later come to be known by members of her company and closest friends, describes three major chronological periods in her life. They are the "learning period," or the years between 1926 and 1939 spent at the University of Chicago and in the West Indies through the starting of the first black concert dance company; the period of "touring the world" which lasted from 1939 to 1967; and the period spent in East St. Louis, the *now* period.

The learning period consisted mainly of time spent off and on at the University of Chicago. In 1934, Dunham, aided by her teacher, Ludmila Speranzeva, formed a company of seven female dancers which performed at the Chicago World's Fair. The small company was a hit. Because of its success and because there were always dancers willing to accept her new ideas in choreography, Dunham continued to perform and choreograph both as a solo artist and with a company.

After eighteen months of study and travel in the West Indies, Dunham returned to Chicago and realized that the whole period of her life that had included the Cube Theater Club, as well as her associations with Ruth Page and Mark Turbyfill, was over. She wanted to teach again but, due to racial discrimination, finding a studio in mid-Chicago was actually impossible. Her good friend and teacher, Speranzeva, rented a studio for Katherine in her own name so she could begin to give lessons.

Then the seduction of the difficult audience of the black upper class and whites began. Chicago blacks still thought people of the West Indies were anthropologically a few levels above anthropoids. On the other hand, whites had to be convinced that blacks were out of the minstrel show and *Black Birds* (an all-black vaudeville production) period of development. In her performances, Dunham joined together a uniqueness of music, a richness of visual and stage design, and gorgeous costumes. Because she created choreography with the eye of an anthropologist and the soul of an artist, her performance, a culmination of these two assets, hit the audience with an even greater impact.

In 1935, the Works Progress Administration (WPA) was established by the government. It was the first program in the United States to subsidize the arts, and one of its more significant features was to give the artist a chance to work in his own medium and be paid. More important, it helped bring the country out of the Great Depression. Many works of art that were created at that time are today still very much a part of our culture. Not only did black visual artists of the period produce a lasting monument to their art such as the oil paintings and sculptures of Sargent Johnson and Thelma Street, but the black playwrights produced exciting works for the theater which, although not as widely performed today, included Hall Johnson's *Run, Little Chillun!* Orson Welles, the white actor-director, directed the black *Haitian Macbeth*.

The WPA had a department for writers and playwrights. In 1938, after her studies abroad, Dunham showed the director of the Writers Project a script for her book *Journey to Accompong* and convinced him that she would be an asset to the position of leader of the department. Once the door was open, she then outlined what she would like to do. She would use the writers Frank Yerby, Nelson Algren, and a fellow anthropologist, Mary Fuji, in a communal research project based on a paper she had submitted to the University of Chicago on the relationship between the social, economic, and racial deprivations of people and their need to belong to religious cults. The aim of the project would be to prove that, under the stresses of oppression and need, more cults sprang up and became successful. The research would center around new religious cults that had appeared in and around Chicago and Detroit, and included as examples not only Father Divine, the prophet Elijah, the Black Muslims, and a separate cult, the Moslims, but also Pentecosts, Seventh-day Adventists, and the Spiritualist, Aimée Semple McPherson.

Dunham credited her success with the WPA to recommendations from professors who knew of her financial difficulties and to the writing that had been necessary to fulfill her fellowship. More important, she felt her acceptance was due to the fact that she had been ready with "a plan." The assignment lasted for nine months.

Soon after she joined the WPA, rumors began to circulate that the Writers Project would be shut down, so she applied for the position of leader with the Federal Works Theater Project. Again, she went in with a plan of action, a ballet entitled *L'Ag'Ya*, which, along with two other ballets, had been hired by the Federal Theater as part of the "Ballet Fedré" before Dunham's association with the Writers Project.

L'Ag'Ya, which Dunham choreographed, produced, and performed in, was based on a Martinique fighting dance and set in a fishing village where she had lived. She herself had written the narrative. The ballet included authentic West Indian dance movements and brilliant costumes and was cast with WPA members whose previous occupations were cooks, maids, chauffeurs, laborers, etc. Since the fishing village where Dunham had done her research was composed of all sorts of people–fat, thin, short, tall, old, and young–*L'Ag'Ya* was well suited to the needs of her group which at that time was composed of many diverse body types.

During the same period Dunham created one of her few solo numbers under the auspices of the Chicago Art Institute; it was performed at the Goodman Theatre. A young woman comes down from the hills to sell pineapples, passes a hut, and hears music she will later dance to. She carries her shoes because she means to save them for the city. When she gets to town, she imagines herself as she will be that evening, at the Palais Shoelecher Dance Hall. The rhythm moves her body in a seductive hip swing. This dance was named the *Biguine*. Only Dunham's feelings for total theater successfully brought this West Indian atmosphere to the stage.

From her research in the West Indies, Dunham had brought

back records, authentic drums of all sizes, and rhythms she had recorded on an old Edison cylinder recorder lent by Herskovits. Studying authentic songs and rhythms, the dancers and musicians were able to completely capture the Caribbean sound and style.

While in the West Indies, Dunham had constantly thought of the theater. Not only did she return with samples of costumes and accessories, but she brought them back in quantities large enough to dress the company for years. The male dancers wore original fishermen's hats from Martinique; the female dancers wore the *haute taille* or high-style Martinique dresses worn at festivals, carnivals, and grand balls which resembled the Empire costume worn by Josephine, Napoleon Bonaparte's wife and a Martiniquaise. These were draped, flowered, high-waisted, full-skirted dresses worn over an abundance of lace petticoats.

According to the style in which they were tied, elaborate head-dresses had certain significance. Women of Guadeloupe wound their ties into a small fan shape in the front. To show they were married, older women in Martinique wore starched madras ties with two or three points made of squared, starched madras cloth, imported from Madras, India, then pleated and dried either on their own heads or on head forms. Single women wound their ties to great heights and each time they were worn, retied them. After doing research on various tribal distinctions on the basis of their head ties, Dunham learned that Haitian women tied their scarves in the back of their heads. In contrast, similar to a custom she had observed in Martinique, the American southern black wore ties fastened in the front.

As Dunham began to feel secure as a choreographer, she realized that she had only begun to draw on her great wealth of experiences in the West Indies. The process of weeding from the company those individuals whose skills were too amateur for her purposes took about a year. By 1939 there were fifteen dancers, the ensemble Dunham considered her first professional company.

Her first company included no preset goals or rules other than those that grew out of necessity. Her previous training and discipline gained from the Anthropology Department at the University of Chicago were helpful. Even the part-time job at the Hamilton Branch Library contributed by teaching her punctuality through the daily routine of signing in and out to work. Thus the most natural form of discipline grew in relationships between company members. Living and working together seemed to necessitate certain rules for survival.

Just as her first company of black dancers were enjoying their initial stages of success, John Pratt, a tall, slim, handsome, blond, born of American parents in Canada, entered Katherine Dunham's life. A soft-spoken, gentle man, with a wit that made him interesting to be with, Pratt had first heard of Dunham while she was still in the Caribbean and had admired her work.

A talented costumer, painter, and commercial fabric designer who had also worked with the Theater Project, Pratt had had several one-man shows in Chicago and two in New York when finally he met Dunham at a party at Paul Schofield's home. They first began to see each other to discuss problems connected with the theater. Later their common work interests blossomed into a genuine need to see each other on a personal basis and to be together. Although co-workers at the Theater Project did not readily accept the "mixed" racial relationship, Dunham and Pratt didn't care and ignored their gossip.

When Pratt heard that the supervisor of the Theater Project had decided either to greatly shorten or throw out Dunham's *L'Ag'Ya*, he was upset because he realized how hard she had worked on the piece. Pratt knew that it would distress her to change it in any way. The same evening he went to her home to tell her the news and to help her figure out a way to save the ballet. It was saved, but more so, his growing concern over Katherine's feelings made him realize how important she was to his life.

One Sunday while they were still courting, Pratt and Dunham decided to visit Katherine's parents in Joliet. It was a very hot day, so Katherine suggested he take off his shirt and sunbathe in the back yard in a protected area. The shocked look on Annette Dunham's face let them immediately know her opinion of their relationship. Annette was horrified that Katherine would have Pratt sit in her back yard without a shirt—"What would the neighbors say?"

Clearly Annette was upset because Pratt was white, but even more so because it was evident her daughter cared deeply for him. Finally, Katherine was forced to take a stand on her relationship with Pratt. She told Annette that she would not return to Joliet to visit until Annette regarded Pratt as her fiance. After a few weeks, Annette changed her mind. As she came to know Pratt, she liked him and they became very close. Until the end of Annette Dunham's life, on the occasions when her daughter would be abroad working and unable to leave, Pratt would come to care for Annette and stay by her side. In the last three months of her life he often relieved the night nurse, staying close to her up to the time of her death by old age in 1958.

After a courtship that lasted two-and-a-half years, Katherine Dunham and John Pratt were married on July 10, 1941.

In the late thirties Dunham's company became the first dance troupe to play opera, concert, and nightclubs in the same time period. Soon after the Federal Works Theater Project closed in 1939, Dunham decided to appear at the Sherman Hotel in Chicago on the same bill with Duke Ellington and Raymond Scott who were starring in the Panther Room. She went to the owner–director, Ernest Byfield, and convinced him that her company should be an attraction. The show consisted of American black dances such as *Barrelhouse*, *Flaming Youth*, *Floyd's Guitar Blues*, and *Cakewalk*, which were danced in shoes, but also included the *Rara Tonga* and *Bolero* which were danced barefoot. Byfield was upset. How could they dare to dance barefoot in his exclusive supper club? Dunham convinced him that carefully made-up feet with toe straps made to look like thonged sandals would not offend his patrons. Finally he agreed. They were a success, and the first black concert dancers to appear in a nightclub.

In spite of Dunham's many initiatives in the field of concert dance, she still carried the enormous burden of reeducating an audience whose only previous exposure to black dance had been in the "Chittlin' Circuit"* of the early 1900s which included such artists as Bill "Bojangles" Robinson, Bert Williams, and "Peg Leg" Bates, the one-legged black tap dancer.

In 1939, Warner Brothers filmed the Dunham Company in their first color short, *Carnival of Rhythm*, a production that consisted

---

* The name given to locations in the United States, mainly in the South, that catered to black audiences and performers.

entirely of Brazilian songs and dances. Jean Negulesco was both producer and director. At the time the company was still performing *Cabin in the Sky* at the Biltmore Theater in Los Angeles.

During the shooting, they noticed a conference among several rather distinguished looking men, and later found out that someone had gone to the Brazilian Embassy and said, "Are you going to let these colored people represent Brazil?" As a result, several embassy officials decided to watch the filming. The diplomats themselves were of mixed racial background and thus representative of one of Brazil's major races. After the viewing, they said that they were charmed and pleased to see this presentation of the art of their country.

When she did the film *Star Spangled Rhythm* in 1942, starring the comedian Eddie "Rochester" Anderson, Dunham had a disagreement with the production company. She had only one spoken line and some dancing. The producer wanted her to say, "You ain't only classy, you is Haile Selassie." She refused to say "You is"; the two finally agreed on her saying *"You're* Haile Selassie."

A misunderstanding that worked in her favor occurred when she was asked to choreograph the movie *Pardon My Sarong*, starring Bud Abbott and Lou Costello. The producer said he understood she was an authority on Tahiti. Although she was certain he had mistaken Tahiti for Haiti, she needed the job and quickly went to the library to check through all of the *National Geographics*. She then canvassed Hollywood for every Samoan, Tahitian, or Hawaiian dancer to integrate into her troupe. She insisted on lavish sets with huge stone monuments, and the scene became a smashing success.

During a trip to New York in 1939 to perform at the Ninety-second Street Y.M.H.A., the Dunham Company attracted the attention of impressario Louis Schaefer. Through the intervention of Mary Hunter, who had been a director at the Cube Theater in Chicago, he invited them to dance at New York's Windsor Theater on weekends when its show, *Pins and Needles*, was not appearing.

They performed at the Windsor thirteen weekends in a row, launching them on a concert career that started at the top. The shows *Tropics* and *Le Jazz "Hot"* opened on Broadway. (Much of *Le Jazz. "Hot"* is now incorporated in Dunham's current choreography, *Americana*.) Dunham received star treatment, including her name on the marquee, a full-size picture in the front showcase, and exceptionally good press.

In 1940 on Broadway, and later on tour, Dunham and her troupe appeared in the musical *Cabin in the Sky*, starring Ethel Waters. George Balanchine, the director, shared the choreography with Dunham.

By now Pratt had become her costume and personal wardrobe designer for all her productions. Along with being designer for Dunham's stage shows and movies, he designed for such stars as Hermione Gingold, Ruth Page, Agnes de Mille, Jerome Robbins, Marian Van Tyle, and Miriam Makeba. He had the ability to produce costumes of exquisite color and design without sacrificing their basic authenticity. His sets were unsurpassed. Audiences who were fortunate enough to see the Dunham Company at that time still reminisce about his fabulous jet-beaded curtain set within bamboo frames. The combination of his costumes and sets coupled with her artistry as dancer and choreographer became the secret of the Dunham Company's success.

Stormy Weather, in 1943, was one of Dunham's better-known movies, due to the outstanding dance sequences. The film also starred Lena Horne.

During World War II, Pratt was stationed in Virginia. Every weekend his life as a drab military man was magically transformed to that of the gifted designer of a very glamorous, successful dance company. It was a hectic schedule: He would drive to Washington, D.C., then take a train to New York to rework costumes, then reverse the process in order to be back in Virginia before his weekend pass expired. Before joining the company on tour he was in the army for two years.

Though confident about her Broadway success, Dunham was troubled by the possibility that it wasn't a dignified avocation for a research anthropologist. What would the university think? There were periods when she mused guiltily, "I wish there were a way to pay back the money I received from the Rosenwald Foundation."

Happily, her thoughts were never those of the Foundation's

board. In fact, one of the Stern family, Alfred, told her, "We are so proud of you." Nevertheless, this feeling of guilt plagued her constantly throughout her performing career. She even expressed her feelings to Robert Redfield, Dean of Anthropology at the University of Chicago, who finally told her, "Why not do both?"

After much guidance and soul-searching, Katherine made the decision to work on her master's degree at the University of Chicago rather than at Northwestern. If she had chosen to work with Herskovits at Northwestern, she would never have continued her career as a choreographer and dancer. Although she knew that she upset many people with this decision, dance for her was a spiritual, physical, and psychological *necessity* that could not be replaced by a career dedicated solely to anthropological research.

Dunham knew that because there had been no company like hers before, dancers' training had been in the contemporary forms of dance only. Teaching her students to move in the primitive style she favored soon became a real problem. Dunham would examine a movement and say, "This is restrictive—let me take this another step forward. Let me see how this can be used. Ballet will not fulfill this, modern won't, what will?"

As a black dancer, she knew ballet was not the next logical step. Physical anthropology had shown her a physical difference existed in the structure of people depending on their race. Although she knew that she could have adapted a ballet base, the great wealth of material, beauty, and rhythm that by now had become such a part of her life seemed to oppose the somewhat frozen torso and highly stylized arm positions of ballet which, as a result, didn't seem the correct foundation for the needs of the primitive style of movement. Thus she would automatically draw on the primitive. All this time, the Dunham technique, which she defined as "a series of forms or exercises derived from primitive rhythms and dance," was developing.

As Dunham created her technique, she first established the isolation, then progressed through various forms of elevations and extensions, all of which developed from the primitive style of moving.

FUNDAMENTAL

All Movements Done at the Barre

Presses into the barre   Feet are parallel, while the body leans into the barre with a straight torso.

Body rolls   With the back parallel to the floor, the body rolls up starting from the base of the spine, curving up through to the head, then back to a starting position.

Drop and recover   This movement combines the motion of swinging the body down to the floor from the hips with body rolls. It begins with the feet flat, followed by pliés and relevés.

Legs   Leg swings are done freely from the hip with a relaxed foot. Leg whips are a ripple in the leg that starts from the hip and ends at the heel.

Extensions   The free leg starts with a bent knee and extends through the toe to a squared foot.

Up and over   The most complete single technique. The entire body is involved in a rolling movement that starts from a standing position and continues to a deep plié and is followed by contractions, followed by a release of the spine which ends at the starting position.

Arms   Arms are curved, parallel to the floor. The center of the palm is also held parallel to the floor, so that the whole arm seems to rest on an imaginary table.

All these movements have variations within the Fundamental; there are also separate variations according to style and influences.*

Variations of Style

Lyrical   Softens all movement and uses the feet in a slightly turned-out position.

Karate A and B   A strong influence of oriental movement is present. (These movements were created during Dunham's 1958 tour to Japan.) The Karate has a more sharp and angular style, but the Fundamental is still the theme.

All Movements Done Away from the Barre Are Usually Performed in the Center of the Room

Isolation   Head moves to the front, back, and sides, and then in continuous circles

---

*To the present Dunham continues to expand on the variations of her technique.

Shoulders move up, down, front, back, and in circles
Rib cage moves front, back, sides, and in circles
Hips move in contractions, releases, and in circles

Progressions
The term used for a movement pattern done across the floor.

*   *   *

The whole concept of dance-isolation as technique, which is
current now, grew out of Dunham's school. "Isolation" is the ability
to move one part of the body while keeping the other parts stationary (e.g., the right shoulder moving front and back while keeping the
left shoulder still). Isolation came from primitive movements.
Dunham explains the sources of "isolation breakdown" as follows:
head and neck movements, from the Pacific islands; torso and arm
movements, from Africa and the West Indies; toe and feet movements, from the Haitian Combite, a field work dance. (A combite is
best described as it relates to the early American barn-raising parties.
A homeowner had a massive job to do on his land and called on his
neighbors to assist. He furnished the food. The difference, however,
is that a Haitian combite is a work party that is done to the beat and
snap of a leader with a drum or some percussive instrument. When
the job is completed, it is followed by much eating, dancing, and
socializing. The movements of the combite are rhythmical and
appear to be a beautiful dance.)
Once the company mastered Dunham's technique, the style and
skill of the choreography became a natural way of moving. The
excitement of seeing one part of the body moving in isolation to one
rhythm while the feet moved in an entirely different rhythm always
left audiences wanting more.
Specific techniques require different physical postures. An
example of this can be found by contrasting the torso in classical
ballet which is lifted and usually moved as one unit with the Haitian
movement, *Yonvalou*, the dance of humility and assurance. This
dance to the serpent *Damballa*, the Haitian *vaudun* god, begins at
the base of the spine by contracting or tucking under the hips in an
upward tilt. Like a ripple in a pool of water, the movement starts
to follow up the spine to the neck and finishes at the neck and head,
only to start again in the hips in an unbroken circuit. The rippling

movement of the torso is done in five levels, from a standing-up position through various lowered postures until in the lowest level both knees are on the floor and one is kneeling. Until the fourth

Yonvalou

level, when the dance goes to relevé, or the heels lift, the feet are flat. According to the insistence of the drummers who play a rhythm consisting of slaps and rolls on the drum head, the various levels may be interrupted at any time, to have the dancers *feint*, or break. The *feint* is an upright movement to release the body and open it up to receive the *loa*, or spirit. It is not performed as a rhythmical movement, but as a stagger that lets both the arms and the head swing at will. Sometimes it is performed with one foot firmly planted on the floor while the body pivots around the stationary foot. It is often from the *feint* position that a *hounci* initiate becomes "possessed" or "mounted" by the *loa*. When a possession takes place, the mounted person becomes that spirit. If it happens to be the god Damballa, symbolized by the snake, the mounted person begins to move and crawl, performing snakelike movements.

Often Dunham has been called upon to defend her choice of the term "primitive rhythms." The title has always been linked with her dance, and to change its terminology would weaken both her philosophy and reputation. Some say she should call her dance technique "third-world percussion." She has said that this title would not be accurate since technically "primitive" implies a people without a written language, a people who live in their original tribal state, which differs greatly from either folk or urban society structures. Cult or primitive dances are not dependent on a unified folk society to be danced; the primitive rhythms they use are basic. Contrasts to the cult or primitive dance would be the *Meringué*, Haiti's national social dance, which is urban. The *Bamboche* and *Carnaval* are considered folk dance events.

Today Dunham looks on her period of "touring the world" which lasted from 1939 to 1967 as a concentrated exposure to business. During these years her company visited fifty-seven countries and geographic subdivisions and seldom performed in America. At this point, she realized that she had chosen her career, and there was no turning back. She had learned enough to secure work, either alone or with partial or full company, and had the responsibility of simultaneously filling many roles—not only that of dancer, but of producer, business administrator, artistic director, and star.

Throughout her long career she remained enchanted with the blues of Chouteau Street in St. Louis and State Street in Chicago. Streets like these were situated in the heart of all black neighborhoods and were social gathering places where many jazz greats met and improvised some of the finest music of our times. Often, spectators would be moved by the soulful sounds to impromptu dance, either solo or with a partner, to the delight of onlookers. *Barrelhouse*, as well as another work, *Floyd's Guitar Blues*, in which she and a partner danced around a company guitarist named Kokomo, were inspired by these neighborhoods.

Dunham says, "This is a part of my artistic and creative expression that will be with me always. I cannot think of myself as choreographer and performer unless I use this part of the black experience, which is so deeply rooted in me."

When *Cabin in the Sky* toured in 1939–40, the company made many friends in Los Angeles and San Francisco. Dunham's good friend Howard Skinner, director of the San Francisco Symphony, proved to be a great help in establishing them in the Bay Area. He asked them to appear with the San Francisco Symphony, and San Francisco became a temporary home base where Dunham not only established a temporary school, but taught classes and choreographed as well.

Today, in remembering the company's appearance with the San Francisco Symphony while Pierre Monteux was guest conductor,

Paquita Anderson, the company pianist, and Dale Wasserman, the company manager, Dunham laughs. Anderson didn't know the difficulty of expanding music scored for small orchestra to symphonic-size orchestration, but rehearsed the symphony up to curtain time, and the company's first appearance with it was a great success.

The company also danced in Carmel, an exclusive West Coast community and temporary residence of Langston Hughes, the poet. Hughes, who had known Dunham since the Cube Theater Club days in Chicago, greatly admired her company and was instrumental in arranging their appearance there.

Often Dunham accepted jobs for a mini-company that performed without her in order to financially maintain the main company. A job at La Fiesta, a popular Mexican-style nightclub in San Francisco, was such an occasion when, with a small company, Talley Beatty and Janet Collins danced, and Marie Bryant, a San Francisco singer, sang Dunham's songs.

While they were based in San Francisco, Sol Hurok saw the company and later became their impressario. In 1944, Hurok decided to cut costs by reducing sets and the number of orchestra members required for Dunham's performances. This was his usual policy after the second or third year a company toured. However, Dunham had strong feelings about his stripping the rich scenery John Pratt had designed. She felt that patrons, in returning to theaters where they had once experienced lavishly staged shows, would not accept a black velvet curtain for scenery and maybe two pianos in place of an orchestra. She knew the change just wouldn't work. Not only would her audience be disappointed; she wouldn't be happy. Therefore, she did what had been heretofore unheard of among companies managed by the great impressario—she bought her contract from Hurok, paying for it in installments over the years. Still, they remained close friends until his death in 1974.

After touring America and Canada with Hurok, the company returned to Broadway in *Carib Song*, a show set in Trinidad. Some time had passed since *Cabin*, and Dunham was happy that *Carib Song*, a true story and a show that was, like so many events in her life, ahead of its time, gave her the opportunity to sing and act again. "Imagine these colored people on the stage speaking in clipped English dialect," a critic said.

"We had worked so hard to be correct in every way, especially in our Trinidad British dialect," Dunham answered.

Although *Carib Song* was one of her favorite productions, it didn't run very long. After *Carib Song* the company appeared in a Billy Rose revue which was short-lived, and as a result of both productions, Dunham once again found herself in a difficult position financially. She realized that it might have been easier to perform with the security of Hurok's backing, and many times she reflected on her wisdom in buying back his contract.

In its use of racially mixed casts for its productions, the Dunham Company was ahead of its time. There was no plan to integrate or not integrate; it just happened. She attracted all sorts of people who came to fill a human need, to move their bodies. Although Dunham did not realize the uniqueness of it, the company remained basically black. At the times when all its members were black it was due to circumstances, since some dances would not be convincing if members of other races participated. For example, *Choros*, a Brazilian-inspired dance choreographed in the early forties, was done by mulattos or whites, if they were in the company and had sufficient ballet training to perform it. In contrast, *Rites de Passage*, an African puberty dance, would not have been believable unless performed by blacks. Even if dancers were non-black, they did not look out of place if they learned the primitive style. Dunham says, "Technique is one thing, but 'style' makes for cohesiveness, and even if the dancers were non-black, they wouldn't stand out as being different."

The shows had different themes, which gave her titles: *Tropics*, *Le Jazz "Hot"*, *Bal Negre*, *Bamboche*, and sometimes just Katherine Dunham and her company of dancers, singers, and musicians.

In 1940, Dunham established a school in Isadora Duncan's old New York studio located in the Caravan Hall. In 1944, the actress–dancer Eartha Kitt was among the dancers auditioning in that studio who later joined the company.

In a series of studio parties called Boule Blanche, the name of a dance hall in Fort-de-France, Martinique, people danced the *Biguine* most of the night. The parties were a great success and included as guests Broadway stars who came to watch the Dunham Company entertain. The parties were given every three months. As word of the parties got around, the Forty-second Street studio became too small; as a result, they had to rent a larger hall.

For eighteen months to two years after the Broadway closings, Dunham worked to establish a school of performing arts, applied skills, and humanities in New York. She had heard that Lee Shubert wanted to present her in a one-woman show. She was not a soloist and therefore preferred to have some members of her company present at all engagements. She refused Shubert, knowing full well that he owned the theater building on Forty-third Street, just off Broadway, where she had hoped to establish her school. After she persuaded him to lease the theater's top floor, which once had been the *George White's Scandals'* rehearsal hall, he let her rent from him at a ridiculously low price. Since John Pratt was in the army in Europe at the time, she employed another designer, a Viennese decorator, who designed the school in brilliant colors.

Those were pioneering years for a new kind of dance academy. The company worked in a large, beautiful, bright studio which included a number of rooms: a children's department, a percussion department, and a large ballet room for demonstrations. Dunham's dance academy later became one of the first studios to be given exchange credit by Columbia University and New York University.

"Papa" Henry Augustine, a Haitian, was the chief drummer for the school and the company, as well as Dunham's Haitian folklore consultant. His percussion demonstrations were exciting, causing the Forty-third Street building to become known for its "Sunday shows." The performances were really a combination of classes, demonstrations, and rehearsals that started in the morning and continued late into the night. Everyone wondered where the high energy of the performances came from.

Although Dunham's classes never completely paid for themselves, they attracted a stream of interesting people—actors like Marlon Brando and José Ferrer, the designer Rudi Gernreich, as well as dancers Arthur Mitchell and Peter Gennaro. Impressarios and managers came each week; likewise ambassadors and dignitaries from South American and Central American countries were in attendance because they felt comfortable in the unusual surroundings. Dunham's studio was the place to be.

Dunham never operated a simple dancing school. She believed performing artists must know more than their own skills. She knew they needed exposure to other stage crafts, and many times stated, "A well-rounded performer should be a well-rounded person." Often she wondered if her own career was successful due to the fact she had been exposed to people in the humanities like Robert Hutchins, President of the University of Chicago; Howard Skinner of the San Francisco Symphony; Paul Robeson, the black singer; Erich Fromm, the writer and psychoanalyst; her professors, and others.

In 1945 her company became the first large troupe, black or white, to appear in Las Vegas. In Vegas, discrimination was a major problem for all traveling black entertainers. The company opened at the El Rancho Hotel and had a very successful run. Although blacks could entertain in hotels, they weren't allowed to sleep in them. Some places didn't even let their black star attractions eat in their kitchens. Although Dunham was able to secure a reservation, her company had to stay on the other side of the tracks in an area reserved for blacks. However, she was able to persuade the management to let her company have meals at the hotel, which caused leading black citizens of Vegas to come as a group to Dunham and demand that she break the hotel's segregation ruling. Dunham felt that, as residents of Vegas, it was the citizens' duty to put demands on the management instead of leaving to her, a temporary employee, the responsibility of being the management's conscience. After she united with the community, barriers were relaxed.

Also in 1945, the company appeared at Ciro's in Hollywood, so successfully that Ciro's became a second home. The company also accepted other club engagements. New management saw them and booked them for a nine-month tour of *Bal Negre*, which culminated in a return to Broadway. This return was, again, brief due to a newspaper strike that curtailed publicity, but the show did attract two European producers, Felix Marouani and Fernard Lumbroso. Then Dunham's friend Doris Duke, the tobacco heiress, invited the company to Mexico, and they went under a contract with Teatro Americano, which was run by three young Americans. There for six months the company rehearsed and Dunham choreographed new works. In 1947 they appeared in Mexico City and Guadalajara, where

Dunham did anthropological research on Mexican life-styles. Her continuing sense of guilt over not becoming an anthropologist drove her to do scholarly work whenever the opportunity presented itself. While in Mexico she went to Veracruz, did more research, and later choreographed the ballet *Veracruzana*. At that time the company was visited by President Alemán of Mexico, who congratulated Dunham on her ability to capture the spirit of Veracruz in dance.

After the completion of the Mexican tour, Katherine welcomed a booking to appear at the Prince of Wales theater in London in June 1948. The company was scheduled for three weeks and stayed three months, described by the press as the "darlings" of Europe. They appeared as an unsubsidized art product in the Near and Far East, Europe, Mexico, Africa, all of the countries of South America, and Haiti and Jamaica in the Caribbean. Royally received by the whole world, they performed on television and in operas, made records and movies, and even appeared in such unlikely places as bullrings in Spain and the south of France.

During a performance in Amsterdam in 1951, Dunham received the shocking news that her beloved brother Albert had died of a brain tumor. Over the years they had remained very close, and she was at a total loss. He had died a brilliant scholar.

It was during this period of travel in Europe that she established a deep friendship with the noted art historian and critic, Bernard Berenson. Their friendship extended over a period of ten years and intellectually provided a great stimulus to her art. Although their very first meeting got off to a bad start because she arrived late, the chemistry was right and both found in each other a positive formula for closeness. Automatically the sharing of very private thoughts and desires inspired an impressive ten-year correspondence between Katherine and "B.B.," as she fondly called him, from his residence "I Tatti" near Florence. As a person, Berenson was extremely important to Dunham and the deep love that grew between them helped her through some very low points, not only in her private life, but in the life of the company.

Berenson inspired her to write. At first, since he was no longer able to leave his villa, he asked her to write him detailed impressions of her tours. By reading her letters he could experience travel once again through her feelings conveyed in letters. His encouragement inspired her to write *A Touch of Innocence* while she was in Japan in 1958. As she completed each chapter, she mailed it to Berenson who sent back comments. Once he said, "Always remember that your transition from your deepest expression on stage to your deepest expression in writing is like making love, and you are making love to a vast humanity either in theater or in writing." Because today she sees writing as physical pleasure, she has often remembered these words.

Dunham's association with the State Department began in the early 1950s when it decided to send representative American artists to foreign lands as "ambassadors" of freedom and understanding. Already the Dunham Company had toured the major countries of the world and wherever they performed had earned respect and a dignified position in the arts. For a long time they tried to officially represent the United States, but the State Department would not hear of it. Unofficially her dancers were cited as "artistic and cultural representatives" of the United States.

As a result of their unofficial status, Dunham couldn't convince the State Department to give them support or subsidy, and when it did decide to give money it was to a Harlem musical jazz group. Dunham was very upset and provoked. Even today, after being obliged to travel to the Far East and South America without State Department aid, she senses a deep injustice.

When the company appeared in Australia in 1957, a representative of the Chinese Opera asked Dunham's impressario if her company could visit Red China. Chinese artists had attended her shows night after night and the representatives felt Chinese people would love them. Dunham's request to tour China was obstinately refused by the U.S. ambassador who said, "You can go if you want to lose your passport and pay $10,000 fine per person." She thought the ambassador's response unjust, especially since the company had been invited by the Chinese government to be guests of the country. Then, in the late sixties, Dunham felt bitter when the United States claimed that their ping pong team was the first breakthrough in communication with Red China.

The State Department later gave the Dunham Company a strange blackball or censorship. When Dunham was in South America about to open her show with an impressario who had invested private funds in the group, a similar attraction authorized by the State Department arrived and sent tickets to the American ambassador, requesting him to attend their opening which occurred on the same night as that of the Dunham Company. Naturally, the ambassador had to attend the government-endorsed affair. This happened repeatedly not only in Montevideo, Uruguay in South America, but also in Greece, Lebanon, Australia, and Europe. It happened so often that Dunham knew it was not by accident. This attitude on the part of the State Department hurt the Dunham Company very much. Although she personally saw letters of complaint from the ambassadors in Australia and other countries about the nonsubsidizing of her company, it did no good. The problem remained very serious.

Dunham also tried to get support from the State Department for her company to entertain U.S. servicemen. Once again State's response was negative. When the troupe finally went to Tokyo to entertain, it meant that the company dancers, who were receiving very good salaries, would be taking a payroll cut down to six dollars a day. The crew, which was solidly union, would not work for less than union scale, so it meant that the difference would be made up out of Dunham's personal funds. Even when she proposed to the State Department a tour encompassing a five to fifty-five member cast with full musical orchestration for a five to one hundred-and-ten piece symphony, no help came.

In 1963 her brother-in-law Davis Pratt, a professor in the Design Department of Southern Illinois University, Carbondale, convinced the Fine Arts Department that her archives should be established there and that she should be an artist-in-residence. Although the University of Texas was also interested, Illinois was her home and seemed a more fitting location to house her history. So, from 1964 to 1966, whenever time permitted, she was artist-in-residence at SIU.

In 1965 Dunham resumed a relationship with Senegal, Africa originally begun in 1962 while she was gathering dancers and material for the show *Bamboche.* In Senegal she found that the effect of her company on European whites was documented in reviews, but that its effect on black students was not. On the occasion of her first audience with Senegalese President Leopold Senghor she was told that, when her company first opened in Europe, it had caused a cultural revolution that paralleled their political and economic revolutions. Different people's chiefs-of-state in sub-Sahara Africa had been encouraged and inspired by her formula and format, adding of course material from their own countries.

Dunham's presence in Africa thus opened a new vista for blacks. Afterward when her company performed in Paris, she saw to it that the American Embassy gave free tickets to African students, much to the chagrin of managements since shows were always sold out. Fortunately, the students saw her performances and, on occasions when she would return to Africa for new material, she was received with open arms. The African students recognized her knowledge as well as the cultural, sociological, artistic, and political significance of her work. They felt she belonged to them.

In 1965 Dunham rallied her company together for another appearance in this country at the Apollo Theater, a famous black vaudeville house in Harlem. Dunham instinctively felt that this would be her company's last appearance. They appeared by accident when the act that was originally scheduled cancelled out due to the summer race riots. When they arrived, Dunham sensed that to gather the dancers, rehearse, inspire, protect, baby, and discipline them was too hard. She knew it was no longer her career and that she was no longer receiving the personal satisfaction that made the hardships of being star, producer, and touring with a company worthwhile.

So, in the following year she returned to Africa between such projects as appearing at the Apollo, starting a new school, undertaking a Paris tour, choreographing an Italian show that starred Marcello Mastroianni, and establishing her archives at SIU in Carbondale. She felt that it was logical to align herself with the Festival of Black Arts in Dakar, Senegal, where Senghor had requested that she return as unofficial U. S. ambassador. In 1966 she made three trips as a U. S. specialist.

There were tragic moments on this assignment. She knew that she was acting for the United States and, consequently, resisted the temptation to expose to Africa what she felt were America's true racial attitudes. Instead, she continued to work and kept strong feelings of responsibility toward her country. Still, she possessed an unwillingness to give in to all of its dictates, in recognizing that she belonged to and was surrounded by the black struggle. Not until she returned to the United States after being appointed to a position of technical and cultural advisor in Africa by President Senghor and had taken her present-day assignment in East St. Louis did she realize that her battle against racial injustice had only begun. She thought that the events of discrimination she had experienced on the road were incidental, like living her book, *A Touch of Innocence*. She was equally certain that the results of the labors of her friends during university days would have contributed toward settling the racial question. In Senegal in 1966 she realized that she had aided in spearheading Africa's cultural revolution. Furthermore, she felt that she belonged to the African intellectual complex and wanted to understand and develop with the African country.

After the festival was over, she remained in Senegal to train its National Ballet. She was not happy with the company's objectives; whereas they wanted to work with "new" creative forms, she felt good theater demanded that they recreate from their own authentic cultural heritage. Even if today, in retrospect, she feels their African objectives were right, at that time she was far more interested in being a guide and in building a way for the Senegalese people to find security in living while training and developing their own indigenous resources.

For Dunham, the period of travel and study in the West Indies was a source of many memories and remained a constant reminder of her own African past. After her period of touring the world she would return to Haiti as often as possible to Habitation Leclerc. The mansion still kept intact many remnants of its rich past, including Pauline Bonaparte's white pool with beautiful tiles which still lined the floor of a gazebo-type structure. When Dunham purchased Leclerc in 1949, the land was still covered with tropical plant life of all types: coconut palms, breadfruit, oak, and mahogany trees. So profuse was the plant growth that the estate appeared surrounded by a jungle in the African Congo. Whenever Dunham visited her land, as though choreographing a dance, she carefully planned the planting or uprooting of trees and plants and hired workers for the job. These were tenant farmers who worked the property.

At the time of her purchase, Leclerc was more isolated than it is today. Then, when illnesses occurred that needed immediate attention such as babies born with parasites and farmers who had illnesses in their joints and other minor ailments, Dunham administered first aid. From her early training with Dr. Max Jacobson she had learned how to give injections. (This knowledge was invaluable in assisting members of her company during their periods of extensive touring at times when she would give vitamin B or penicillin injections to ailing dancers.) Once a week Haitian doctors visited Leclerc to help her diagnose, prescribe, and treat patients. In turn she sent for free samples of drugs and vitamins, which became her major source of medicine, from her friend Jacobson in New York.

When word spread to the surrounding villages and mountains that a black American woman was administering free medicine, a clinic evolved. Because of Dunham's respect for folk medicine in addition to more conventional types of treatment, she was trusted by Haitians. One of her patients was a fisherman who came by boat from La Gonave, a trip of about one-and-a-half days by small boat, to be treated. The most prevalent disease she treated then which is still prevalent today was tuberculosis. It was not rare to have a family carry a sick child on a voyage of one or two days until Dunham could treat it. Sometimes Dunham noticed professional jealousy toward her from both the *vaudun* priest and herb medicine doctors. One case in point occurred when she threatened to fire a child's father who worked at Leclerc because he wanted to wrap his sick child in blankets before carrying him up into the hills to an herbalist. The child, who was very ill, was suffering from a high fever due to the combined effects of malaria and parasites. Finally the father was convinced to leave the child under her care. Although this incident placed a great responsibility on Dunham, she cured the child.

For patients with more severe illnesses, Dunham fashioned a kind of isolation unit on the gallery of her home, where she placed her own bed so that she could give round-the-clock medication. If she had to leave, she would place a nurse in charge of the patients. Often they refused the nurse's help and would only allow the black American to administer to their needs.

Dunham has always loved children. Today at Leclerc she pays for the schooling and housing of seven children who were once among the many transients who drifted on and off the property. Habitation Leclerc has always been a sort of asylum where they could come and be welcome. Her biggest challenge was trying to plan what the youths should do when they become of age. Some continued to work on the estate, whereas others moved on.

Dunham and Pratt adopted their only child, Marie Christine, in Paris. Dunham had finished an exciting opening, in 1948, at the Théâtre des Champs-Elysées, complete with several curtain calls and flowers, and excellent press. Many Parisians thought she was from the Caribbean because she sang in the various languages native to that area and because much of her material was West Indian. After reading the following morning's reviews, some nuns at a Catholic nursery in Fresnes, near Paris, decided to contact Dunham. They had just received an infant they believed had Caribbean blood and thought it would be a fine idea if Dunham and Pratt were to adopt the baby. The prospective parents first saw the child when she was nine months old. The company then left Paris to continue their tour and, when the child was fifteen months old, they returned. At first Dunham and Pratt had no intention of adopting her, but after repeated visits to the nursery they became attached to the little girl, and their love for her grew.

Once they had decided to adopt Marie Christine, or "M.C." as she was later nicknamed, wheels of red tape started slowly to roll. During the waiting time, the new parents kept her with them as much as possible. As far as Pratt and Dunham were concerned, M.C. was theirs, although the total legal procedure was not signed and sealed until 1951, when she was four years old.

Later, Dunham asked a psychiatrist what age he thought M.C. should be told that she was adopted. He said that although he trusted Pratt's and Dunham's timing, it should be done before the child reached adolescence and could hear of her adoption from someone else. Therefore, the new parents both began to condition M.C. when she was six or seven years old to the facts of her adoption. They let M.C. know that, even if one was adopted, the parents still really loved and wanted the child. Furthermore, she was selected and not an accident of nature.

Because of the constant touring it was a great responsibility to try to raise a little girl. Whenever possible, M.C. was taken along. A makeshift nursery was constructed in the dressing room backstage where she either slept in a basket or played. As she got a little older she often would try to put on Dunham's makeup and fancy head-dresses. She was very bright and easily picked up the lyrics of most of the songs in the show.

When M.C. became of school age, she had to be left with the Catholic sisters, who saw to her education. M.C. never liked leaving her new parents to go back to school, but Dunham felt it was necessary that she return to the sisters for her basic educational skills. When M.C. was twelve she began to accept her adoption. Even the sisters would talk to her about it. At the same time, she began to be curious about her natural parents. Dunham and Pratt had little information about her mother and nothing about her father. Because they always considered M.C. their own daughter, the identity of her natural parents had never interested them.

M.C. then spent several years in Switzerland, usually at schools for children of parents traveling in the diplomatic corps. School holidays and vacations found her traveling alone from Switzerland to Mexico, Australia, or other parts of the world to meet her parents.

As a parent, Dunham was permissive. She never had success in saying to her daughter, "Do things my way." As a result M.C. could do as she pleased and quickly learned to do things her own way. Dunham remembers a time when M.C. was forbidden to eat chocolate candy due to a slight liver ailment. Chocolate was hidden from her, but on one occasion M.C. found some and bit into it. Little teeth marks were left on the bar, but when Dunham confronted M.C. with the candy, she denied nibbling it. Dunham told her it was better to tell the truth. For Dunham it was a real crisis because she didn't yet know how to get Marie Christine to understand and accept punishment, if there was to be any. Finally M.C. said, "If I tell the truth will you punish me?"

Dunham said, "Well, not if you put it that way, but I think I'll probably let it go if you just tell the truth about it." Frequently their wills would clash in this manner.

People were always curious to know if Marie Christine had any interest in a dance career. Although as a young adult she studied

Dunham technique and enjoyed movement, she also had experienced the unglamorous side of the theater. Emphatically, she made up her mind that she would "have none of it," and at 31 she has stuck to her word. Marie Christine has not embarked on a career as a performer, but in 1978 she opened her own classes of Dunham technique in Rome, Italy.

Show Reminiscences

Often Dunham reflected on her career which had spanned successions of concerts and films alternating with periods of research. She never felt that she had reached the stage of her development where she had done all that she could or had even accomplished all that she should. Although she had reached "a peak" for a black performer in the thirties and forties, she did not wish this summit to limit her in any way. Whereas the ascent of success seemed constant, discouragement, too, came to her in different forms.

Throughout Dunham's earlier career, her company was the target of racial prejudice. While in New York she maintained her own apartment, so she was not directly affected by housing discrimination. On the road it was a different story. Usually an advance person or friend secured accommodations; at other times, having a white husband and secretary made the housing problems easier. But too often housing was refused.

During the late forties and fifties Dunham appeared in Hollywood at the clubs on The Strip, such as Ciro's, The Trocadero, and The Little Trocadero. At this time, to live nearby was purely a practical measure since the only alternative would have been commuting from one side of Los Angeles to the other. Unfortunately, the major black hotels were located on the opposite side of town on a street named Central Avenue in East Los Angeles. Once again, aided by her husband and secretary, Dunham was able to obtain an apartment in a previously unintegrated neighborhood directly across the street from the club.

The company's second nightclub appearance on The Strip was at The Little Trocadero when Felix Young hired Dunham to both produce and star in a musical revue. For contrast, she persuaded Felix to add a singer to the act and remembered having gone with Noble Sissle, the black orchestra leader, to see Lena Horne. Though Horne at that time was still building her career, Dunham was already her great fan. Dunham urged, argued, and finally got Young to okay the idea. (Now she smiles, reflecting on that particular performance, because Lena stole the show.) Each performance was attended by great crowds of movie stars. As the crowds increased, the management placed more tables on the dance floor. The arrangement was great for Horne, since the closeness brought an intimacy that was positive for a singer. But for the dancers it was impossible. Dunham's skirts actually swept over the patrons' heads.

When Lena Horne arrived, she also had housing problems. She had brought along her school-aged daughter whom she wanted to attend a public school that was close to the club. Finally, Dunham was able to find them housing in her own neighborhood, so they too would not be inconvenienced by living on one side of town and working and going to school on the other.

But it wasn't always that easy. Often there would be complaints when Dunham stayed in hotels where blacks weren't allowed. One such segregated hotel was the Mayflower in St. Louis. In retaliation, some members of the lighting and stage crews of the St. Louis theater where she appeared decided that they wouldn't work if a black were allowed to live in a midtown white hotel (or for that matter, any other previously segregated hotel). Because of prior contractual commitments and the threat of union intervention coupled with lawsuits, the disagreement was settled and the show went on. But Dunham didn't move.

Another serious incident occurred in 1954 when the company appeared in Covington, Kentucky across the river from Cincinnati. The Cincinnati unions threatened the hotel where Dunham and her secretary were living. Dunham's usual reaction would have been to take quick action, settle the union dispute, and then move right in.

But she carried the fight to the bitter end, which caused the particular segregation law which had been in effect before to be void.

An even more dramatic example of discrimination occurred during World War II in Lexington, Kentucky when the management of the theater refused to let blacks sit on the main floor. Dunham immediately tried to reach Hurok, her agent, and couldn't. It was the theater's policy to seat blacks in the balcony only. After a heated discussion that held up the show for half an hour, the management gave in and let two or three blacks sit on the main floor. Immediately following the last curtain call, Dunham had the house lights turned on and spoke to the audience: "Right now war is being fought. People the color such as we are going without question to fight the war, giving our lives, and we come to a city like this and find that we cannot have our people seated among you because of color. I will have to say that it is impossible for us to return to you, or appear for you again as much as we would like to, since we see by your response you would like us to come back. But we cannot appear where people such as ourselves cannot sit next to people such as you." Because it was a very emotional and moving experience for her, she doesn't remember what else was said. At the end of her speech, white people seated all over the theater applauded and wept. In the next few days the ticket sales for Marian Anderson, the world-renowned black mezzo-soprano, were changed from segregated to nonsegregated seating.

Today Dunham remembers several instances when the company was touring with Hurok where theaters with histories of segregation, or restricted seating areas (usually in the top gallery of the theater) where minorities were allowed to sit, changed their rules shortly after the company's appearances. As soon as she arrived in a town, Dunham had a routine action she followed. She would pick out a group like the Urban League or the National Association for the Advancement of Colored People and find out if they had had trouble securing tickets, and also where their seats were located. This action was often done late in the afternoon in the short space of time after she arrived in the city before the show that evening began. If she found that blacks were in segregated areas of the theater, she gathered together as many people as possible in a protest rally with the aim of getting them seats in a nonsegregated section. But this was not always an easy solution. Many, fearing repercussions, wouldn't accept tickets. They refused because some were civil service or state workers who were afraid for their jobs. They told her that she'd be moving on after the show, but they would be left with their problems. Dunham said, "If somebody doesn't do it, how will it change?"

The Dunham Company never appeared without at least one black person sitting in a previously segregated area of the audience. In this manner Dunham contributed little by little to breaking down the barriers of racial discrimination.

Rarely did Dunham share her innermost feelings with the company, although sometimes older, closer members sensed her moods. Nor did she publicly share feelings of unrest or sadness, but would say, "It's so easy to be depressed when you have a great responsibility."

One of Dunham's great frustrations was not being able to produce the ballet *Southland* in the United States. Dunham put a lot of work into this ballet, which grew out of an experience of shock and stress in her own life. *Southland* had been commissioned by the Symphony of Chile. While appearing in Buenos Aires, the company had heard about the lynching of an American southern black youth. While touring, Dunham didn't keep up to date with daily happenings in America, and she was not aware that lynchings still took place. But upon hearing the news, she was appalled by its immediacy and felt compelled to do a ballet on the subject. She began with a text that stated as its premise that "a man who loves his country is one who can not only voice its ills, but also see its attractions and strengths." In the opening section of the ballet, the story, narrated to a musical accompaniment, proclaims Dunham's love of all America from border to border, but it cautioned that there was one ill—racial prejudice. With *Southland* Dunham felt she could be an artist who accurately represented the feelings of social change by commenting on the particular lynching incident that to her was both devastating and disappointing.

Southland was mounted in Argentina. It had a script in southern dialect that caused the company to become upset with some of the words they were supposed to say. Dunham felt they would have a better sense of the action and drama if the story was first verbalized; however, in the actual performance of the ballet she deleted the words.

Pratt did fantastic sets and costumes. A huge three-dimensional magnolia tree stood center stage, and the front curtains symbolized the pillars of a southern mansion.

The first scene of Act I opened with a blind beggar standing upstage. A Greek chorus draped in black and seen as a block that performed very little movement stood on one side of the stage.

Julie Belafonte danced the part of a white girl embracing a white man. A lover's quarrel erupts and she is badly beaten. She is left sobbing in the middle of the stage, where she is discovered by a group of young black male field hands. Ricardo Avalos, the lead black male dancer, stops to console her. The other four male dancers and the chorus try to prevent him from helping her since they know serious consequences can result if a black man is caught touching a white woman.

Julie had to act as well as dance to create the illusion of the imagined lynch mob that was forming offstage. She did a powerful series of movements as if to emotionally arouse the imaginary mob to attack and lynch Ricardo. With an alarming show of tension and fear, Ricardo reacted to the mob as he was dragged offstage. Although the actual lynching was supposedly done offstage, Julie's reaction caused it to appear as though it were happening onstage. A red glow to simulate the body burning could be seen in the wings.

The second scene showed the blackened, ragged body of Ricardo hanging from a rope and swinging from a tree. (The first night *Southland* was performed a stagehand failed to place the check on the rope. Thus Ricardo continued to swing like a pendulum until Julie stopped him. After that incident, a check-rope was secured offstage before the performance so the mistake would never happen again.) When Julie and the mob left, the body was taken down by the chorus, who chanted deep, lingering tones. Her trophy was a piece of clothing torn from Ricardo's body. In this scene, Claudia McNeil sang "Strange Fruit," a song made popular by the late singer Billie Holiday. Lucille Ellis, who played Ricardo's black girlfriend, followed the funeral cortege offstage.

Act II was set in a cafe. A long bar covered one wall, and tables were placed in a circle around a small dance floor. As the curtains parted, Dolores Harper sang "Basin Street." One man walked slowly across the stage and angrily threw a knife into the floor. Picking it up, he repeated the action over and over again. (Even though this added a feeling of suspense, the theater management was angry over the marks that were left on the floor.) In the midst of the song, a kind of lowdown, earthy dancing occurred with the couples so close to each other that they appeared to be one sensual slow-moving shape. As the funeral cortege went through, the blues music stopped. The music was then played again, but in a minor key, against the chorus' mourning chant. Dancers and singers then froze, causing the scene to be stamped in the minds of the audience, who by now felt a deep-seated tension and militant reaction that seemed virtually on the point of exploding. At that point the blind beggar, who had been sitting upstage throughout the ballet, became the only one who "saw." He then stood up and, as if seeking help for all his black brothers, reached out to the audience with his hand.

The last scene then changed into a sad, slow yet menacing dance, as very slowly the people returned to their minor-key dancing and drinking.

In Santiago, Chile, the American Embassy asked that *Southland* not be performed, but Dunham insisted. "It must be done. If you don't want it done, you must assure me that this sort of thing is ended in the United States." Of course she knew this was a rhetorical statement, and the company danced *Southland*. On opening night the theater was packed, the audience cried and clapped, but the party of Americans present were terribly embarrassed and left in a huff. Shortly after its opening, Dunham began to have even more problems with the State Department.

Only one paper, which was Communist, ran a review of the dance, and it was excellent. Later Dunham found out that the newsprint for the other papers was owned by the United States, and that their publishers had been instructed to leave out comments on *Southland* whether good or bad, or risk having their newsprint withheld. Today Dunham is still bitter about the State Department's blackballing *Southland*.

When the company arrived in Paris, at a press party for Dunham's concert that was to open the next night, reporters who had heard about the Chilean incident asked if she planned to present *Southland*. After asking the advice of the American ambassador, who was an old friend, Dunham decided to include *Southland* in the concert. She explained that if she didn't do it, right-wing newspapers would say she had been stopped by the American Embassy; on the other hand, if she did do it, she would risk the displeasure of the American government. Americans in Paris were very angry over the performance, but the French gave the company great reviews.

With artistic success and critical acclaim, *Southland* repeatedly played to houses that weren't completely full. Since other shows filled houses, it was temporarily dropped from the repertory. After its failure Dunham felt disappointed to have put so much of her creative energy into a ballet whose message, in dance form, the public could not yet accept. Even Bernard Berenson had voiced his doubts and disapproval over *Southland* being the proper piece for her company and had advised her against its production.

During her performing career, Dunham often worked to the point of exhaustion. Thus, she was frequently plagued with chronic health problems. Another disappointing show remembrance occurred in Bologna, Italy. The company had been touring, and Dunham had refused to admit that she was not well and could not continue without rest. It was winter. Because she had wanted to see the Italian countryside, she was touring Italy by car. Previously, she had suffered symptoms of an influenza virus that could have led easily to pneumonia and had even been given massive doses of penicillin to cure it. On tour, she would visit a different physician in each new town where the company arrived. Ultimately this proved to be disadvantageous to her health, since at each stop a different doctor would prescribe a different antibiotic as the only alternative to bedrest, which she refused to even consider.

Finally in Bologna she realized how very sick she was. A friend who came backstage was shocked to see her looking so ill. Before, in Venice, she had had medical care with a doctor's orders that she should not perform in Bologna. Knowing that she had one free day before the show opened, she proceeded to arrive there by train and

have Vanoye Aikens, her partner, meet it. Aikens then carried her to
a waiting car which sped from the depot straight to the hospital. She
had insisted on this way of getting there because she didn't want
adverse publicity declaring her as sick. She was afraid of word getting
out to the press that she was too ill for the show to open the next
day. Although doctors in the hospital told her that she should not
even consider performing for weeks, Dunham talked her way out of
the hospital, opened the show, and collapsed right onstage. She was
immediately placed in intensive care because an overdose of anti-
biotics had caused uremic poisoning. She was gravely ill, and the
medical staff didn't think she would pull through.

Realizing how sick she was, her secretary Margery Scott called
Max Jacobson, Dunham's friend and physician in New York, to tell
him she was dying. Jacobson answered, "Nonsense," and spoke to
the medical chief. Jacobson then prescribed a new medication in
such massive dosage it shocked the attending physicians. Following
his instructions, the hospital staff administered the medication and,
miraculously, she recovered.

Dunham was then told not to perform for three months to
allow full recuperation. Common sense told her four months would
have felt better, but she had a company to support. Although
company members sympathized with her situation, the unions
demanded that she pay them full salaries, even when, due to sick-
ness, she could not offer them work. She therefore decided that she
couldn't afford to be sick and further harassed Jacobson to find her
restorative medicines, even if he had to send to Switzerland to get
them. The company was due to open in Milan in two weeks. Defying
doctors' orders, Dunham opened the show as scheduled. She knew
she looked ill; her skin had now dried due to the extremely high
fever; and in one week she'd lost sixteen pounds and was continuing
to lose. Nevertheless, she persevered, saying "If you have a performance to do, you just do it, if at all possible."

In foreign cities like Florence, Rome, or Venice, after the show
Dunham and Margery Scott frequently walked in search of out-of-
the-way places to get the feel of the city. In Paris she liked to watch
the market vendors set up their stalls in Les Halles in the early morning. Likewise, marketplaces in Argentina were not only exciting, but

also gave her a knowledge and feeling for what native people were like, which she carried to stage performances such as *Woman with a Cigar*.

Today Dunham possesses what she refers to as "diffused optimism" about the press given to her company. Except for one statement she read in a London paper in the early fifties that stated, "Miss Dunham was charming as ever, but a little plumper, or heavier," her personal press has always been good. (She was five months pregnant at the time.)

Although Dunham was the company's sole choreographer, the dancers often added valuable nonchoreographic input. It was never her intention not to allow others to choreograph, but since the company always seemed to be in a hurry and pushed to get things done, she followed her own strong, sure, creative feelings about choreography and did not choose to involve other dancers. During her career as a performer, she never believed that a real choreographic talent appeared among members of her company. However, now that Dunham and her ex-company members are in a noncompetitive situation, she sees that Lenwood Morris, Clifford Fears, the late Ural Wilson, and others have created valuable works.

Dunham feels that choreography is something most dancers *don't* feel or understand. She thinks that once one has achieved the position of a featured or star performer, as many in her company have done, there isn't enough time to perfect and develop one's performance ability and still choreograph.

After any show a performer experiences what often is termed a "high." A high usually means that one has reached an emotional peak due to the excitement and stimulation of the show. Although the last curtain may come down, the performer doesn't "come down" until much later. *How* the performer comes down varies, but for Dunham the process always began after finding a nightspot to eat and drink. She was never able to eat during the four or five hours preceding a show, and used to envy people like Lucille Ellis who could eat minutes before performing. After each show Dunham was ravenous. In New York, she used to go to Billy Daniels' place in Harlem, cafes on Fifty-seventh Street, or little delis in the Village where one could eat and drink until 1:00 A.M. Since the shows generally closed at 10:30 P.M., by 1:00 A.M. she was sufficiently down from the ecstatic high she experienced during a good performance.

Dunham often talked to Jacobson, her physician, about the "other" feeling of sadness that came with being down which would invariably follow a successful performance. After an unsatisfactory concert she would have disgruntled feelings, make excuses, or be angry, whereas, after a successful show she would be at a high level of excitement, and then wonder, "What happens tomorrow? Will I be able to reach this peak of dancing again?" Dunham believes that a feeling of disbelief and sadness is experienced by many performers when the final curtain comes down.

Applause and favorable press are ways in which a public's appreciation is indicated to the artist, but the tangible and ceremonial acknowledgments are citations and awards. Dunham is especially proud of those received from the Haitian government. In 1948 President Estime presented her the medal of the Chevalier of the Legion of Honor. In 1972, President "Papa Doc" Duvalier made her a Commander, then later, a High Commander, and as a result she became the recipient of a Ribbon and Iron Cross. These citations are very dear to her because they are outward signs that Haitians recognize the love she has for their country, and also efforts she has made at every possible opportunity to make Haiti known and loved by the rest of the world.

In her home in East St. Louis, Dunham has a wall full of other very impressive awards which have been presented by the Benevolent Order of the Black Elks, the University of Chicago, and the Lincoln Academy, as well as various sororities and fraternities. In 1974, she was inducted into the Black Filmmaker's Hall of Fame in Oakland, California and received a proclamation from the mayor of Detroit. Each award or citation demonstrates a kind of regard, respect, and recognition for what she has done. She is still very excited and proud when one of these acknowledgments takes place.*

It was always hard for Dunham to express her feelings about success. Because she dislikes failure and hated to feel that she had failed in anything, she took succeeding for granted. Throughout her career she never failed to show confidence in viewing her achievements. Her measure of accomplishment was never how her work was reviewed, or how the public saw it, but rather how her own critical

---

*On January 15, 1979, Katherine Dunham received the Albert Schweitzer Music Award at Carnegie Hall in New York City during a gala performance by Dunham dancers.

and intuitive nature reacted. Sol Hurok once told her, "Never worry about what critics say—just take a tape measure and measure it."

Dunham's final performance, in 1965 in Harlem's Apollo Theater, was not a well-planned "swan song" with the public told of her retirement in ample time to see her last show; rather, the event was the result of circumstance. In fact, three times previously she had thought her dancing career was finished.*

The first such "closing" occurred in 1950 when, having just recovered from an appendectomy, Dunham remembers sitting before her makeup table in Haiti and asking Ann Grayson, her friend and dresser, if she thought she would sit in front of that mirror any more. Nevertheless, time and again Dunham would find herself seated at the old familiar dressing table, waiting to go onstage.

In 1960 the company temporarily closed in Vienna, leaving Dunham with a deep feeling of disillusion with certain individual co-workers. She had set their achievement marks too high. Looking back, she has reassessed the situation. She knows that the company stayed together only because of great personal sacrifice by all its members. Although some had ways of doing things that she didn't approve of, she still would have had to disband the company. Her deepest disappointment was always the feeling of not having instilled in her dancers her own ideology, which to her had meant success.

The Vienna closing was never meant to be permanent because performing and touring with the company was how she made her living. She had hoped to return to Europe to research and study and perhaps to maintain a smaller company. She didn't feel that the company needed new choreography, just new spirit. It didn't happen. Something was missing.

Then Steven Papich, a new impresario and former student of the Dunham School in New York, asked her to do a new show. They decided to call it *Bamboche*, a Haitian term for "having a good time." The timing was not good, because the show's New York opening coincided with the Bay of Pigs debacle in 1962. People were glued to television and radio; just too much seemed to be going on. Again, Dunham didn't feel the closing was permanent and thought that when the world crisis calmed down the show would continue. At

---

*Members of this company danced once again, along with students of PATC, when, on January 15, 1979, three generations of dancers performed together at the Dunham Gala at Carnegie Hall in New York City.

that time the company included fourteen Moroccans that King Hussan II, an acquaintance since the Dunham Company's earliest North African tour, had sent to appear on the tour. All of the Moroccans stayed two or three weeks longer in New York until finally, Dunham released them to go home. At last she was convinced that, in an impossible situation, it wasn't feasible to hang on. She dismissed her regular company as well, since at the time it was too expensive to keep everyone on salary without backing. When *Bamboche* closed, many of the regular company members were staying in and around New York, and Dunham still did not see this as meaning the end of her company.

Once again she felt a rare freedom from responsibility for people's lives as she'd felt once before in Paris doing the musical *Les Deux Anges* and during her illness in Bologna. She knew that she could finally pull away from the theater and just write, even though she knew it would never be as remunerative as the theater. Gradually this sense of freedom took over.

Today in the Performing Arts Training Center of Southern Illinois University, a group of dancers and musicians under her direction still bear the ties of a company as an extended family, although not as strongly as with her former professional group. The time, the place, and the young people of today are different from the former chemistry. As a result, the total responsibility and involvement that she felt in her earlier companies just isn't present. For instance, she knows that more lenient work attitudes are the *only* way to advance in East St. Louis, and the result makes for a far different group of dancers. Dunham's goal for the small group in the school is not the competition of the professional theater market, but exposure through travel and social awareness that will help their members survive and grow in their personal lives.

After a year in East St. Louis, Dunham was finally able to turn away thoughts of ever returning to the stage. She saw in the work she was doing and in the work yet to be done that she could make a major contribution to the black movement and thus to the humanists of the world.

Ruth Beckford dancing
with the Dunham Company
in Spokane, Washington (*from
the collection of Katherine Dunham*)

L'Ag'Ya, based on a Martinique fighting dance,
1936 (*from the collection of Katherine Dunham*)

Lucille Ellis and Katherine Dunham in *Barrelhouse* (*from the collection of Katherine Dunham*)

Katherine Dunham's million-dollar legs (*from the collection of Katherine Dunham*)

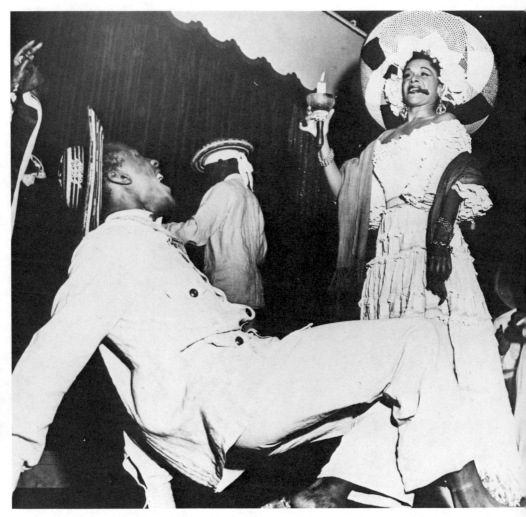

Lady with the Cigar from *Tropics* and *Le Jazz "Hot"*, Amsterdam (*from the collection of Katherine Dunham*)

Katherine Dunham and Vanoye Aikens in *Barrelhouse* (*from the collection of Katherine Dunham*)

KATHERINE DUNHAM

and her Dance Company

8:15 P.M.

Monday, April 19, 1943

MASONIC TEMPLE AUDITORIUM

Presented by

INLAND EMPIRE
EARLY BIRDS BREAKFAST CLUB
SPOKANE, U. S. A.

Program

*

OVERTURE

1. HAITIAN CEREMONIAL DANCES

   (a) Congo Paillette

   Danced chiefly in the spring. perhaps with origins in fertility rites.
   the Congo Paillette is one of those semi-ritualistic group dances now
   performed for social pleasure.

   (b) Younvalou—Rada-Dahomey Cult

   Knife Priests   -   -   -   -   *Talley Beatty, Tommy Gomez*
   A dance sacred to Damballa. the snake god. To the accompaniment
   of snakelike motions the priests execute a ritualistic duel.

   (c) 'Zepaules—Rada-Dahomey Cult

   Hounci   - - - - - - - - - -   *Ruth Beckford*
   Mombo (Priestess) - - - - - - - - -   *Syvilla Fort*
   A Vaudun dance in which a Hounei. one of the lesser initiates. be-
   comes possessed.

2. RUMBA SUITE

   (a) Concert Rumba - - - - - - - - - - -   *Morejon*
   KATHERINE DUNHAM with Collins,
   Williams, Beatty, Marchant

   (b) Rumba with a Little Jive Mixed in - - - - -   *Andre*
   Ellis, French, Gomez

   (c) Diablitos
   Talley Beatty, Tommy Gomez

   (d) Santos Ritual - - - - - - - - - - -   *Anderson*
   Syvilla Fort, Roger Ohardieno

   (e) Pink Scene—Cuban Danzon - - - - - -   *Copeland*
   Lady with the Shoes, KATHERINE DUNHAM

   INTERMISSION

3. RITES DE PASSAGE - - - - - - - - -   *Anderson*

   This can best be characterized as the set of rituals surrounding the
   transition of an individual or group of individuals from one life crisis
   to another. The Ritual period, often at once both sacred and dangerous. is under the guidance of the elders of the community. The
   entire community joins in this critical transition so that the individual may. in a changed status. have a complete rejoining with the
   society.

   The rites dealt with here do not concern any specific community nor
   any authentic series of rituals. They were created to try and capture
   in abstraction the emotional body of any primitive community and to
   project this intense, even fearful personal experience under the important change in status and the reaction of the society during this
   period.

(a) Fertility Ritual
   Maiden in the Community - - - - - *Lavinia Williams*
   Man in the Community - - - - - - *Laverne French*
   In this instance this ritual is associated with marriage or mating.

(b) Male Puberty Ritual
   Boy Initiate - - - - - - - - - - *Talley Beatty*
   Warrior - - - - - - - - - - *Roger Ohardieno*
   The passing from boyhood to manhood by means of formal initiation. The first section portrays the boy's isolation and his vision of
   becoming a warrior. In the second section, masked men of the community, led by the warrior who has appeared in the boy's dream,
   come to take him to the formal initiation. He is both eager and
   afraid.

(c) Death Ritual
   Matriarch - - - - - - - *KATHERINE DUNHAM*
   The wives of a chief mourn his death. Through the intervention of
   the matriarch the defeat of death is accomplished and the life cycle
   continued in the ceremonial ritual of fecundation.

4. RHYTHM INTERLUDE
   Ellis, Gaucho, Candido

5. TROPICS—SHORE EXCURSION - - - - - - *Anderson*
   Woman with a Cigar, KATHERINE DUNHAM

INTERMISSION

6. BRAZILIAN SUITE
   (a) Ciudade Maravilhosa
      Chamber of Commerce.

   (b) Maracatu
      A Brazilian Indian rhythm.

   (c) Bahiana
         KATHERINE DUNHAM
      A samba of the Batuke people.

   (d) Choro
      A musical improvisation.

   (e) Tristeza
      A Toada, Brazilian style of "blues." The women await the
      arrival of the men from the coffee fields.

   (f) "Adeus Terras"
      A slave lament for the African lands left behind. A Macumba
      rhythm.

7. PLANTATION DANCES FROM "BR'ER RABBIT AN' DE
      TAH BABY"
   Interlocutor - - - - - - *KATHERINE DUNHAM*
   Field Hands - *Beatty, Gomez, Marchant, Neal, Ohardieno*
   Couple from Memphis
         KATHERINE DUNHAM, Laverne French
   The corps de ballet appears in the Square Dance, Juba, Jennie
   Cooler, Palmer House, Pas Mala, Ballen' de Jack, Strut and
   Cake Walk.

MEMBERS OF THE COMPANY

LUCILLE ELLIS	TALLEY BEATTY
RUTH BECKFORD	LAVERNE FRENCH
JANET COLLINS	TOMMY GOMEZ
SYVILLA FORT	FRANK NEAL
LAVINIA WILLIAMS	CLAUDE MARCHANT

ROGER OHARDIENO

Costumes Designed by John Pratt

Lighting and Stage Management by Dale Wasserman

Suggestions on minstrel tunes and dances by
Clarence Muse and Lawrence Deas

First Piano—Paquita Anderson   Second Piano—Palmer Johnson
Percussion—Gaucho Vanderhanz and Candido Vicenty

Exclusive Management:
HUROK ATTRACTIONS. INC.
711 Fifth Avenue, New York City
Booking Direction: National Concert and Artists Corp.

L'Ag'Ya, based on a Martinique fighting dance, 1936 (*from the collection of Katherine Dunham*

The Black Witch
of Tenth Street

Tenth Street in East St. Louis could easily be mistaken for a complex for witches of all faiths. A two-lane street with ruts and bumps that have too long gone unattended, its sidewalks have cracks where brave and sturdy weeds have added their greenery to the gray squares. The curbs are high and cluttered with debris from the quick-food stands that dot the landscape. Each block has at least three or four gaping holes where houses stood before the militant outbreaks of the sixties. Now the holes are filled with discarded autos, broken bottles, weeds, and other cast-offs. The holes of some blocks still contain the fire-gutted houses of that period. These old, empty houses look like human skulls. The upstairs windows form the two empty eye sockets; the door frame, without the door, the nose; and the long front porch from wall to wall, the mouth. A perfect setting for a witches colony, but to East St. Louis residents, only one witch lives on Tenth Street, and she is Katherine Dunham.

    Dunham knows that some people believe she is a witch, and that often when out of hearing range she is referred to as "The Black Witch of Tenth Street." Why this title? She doesn't look like a witch. She's a woman who has the presence and graceful movements of a dancer. Neither does she dress like a witch; she is most often seen in navy blue because her Cuban godmother once instructed that it was the color of Katherine's patron saint Yemanja and, hence, Dunham should dress in navy blue, as well. Sometimes she may wear a chic headwrap or go bare-headed, letting her mingled gray, medium-length afro frame her well-structured face. Her abundant jewelry is mostly eighteen carat gold. She wears two or three necklaces and several rings on each hand, sometimes placing two or three of these on her little finger. She is never without the two small gold chameleons pinned on her dress or blouse which are worn together as a protective charm.

Her own two-story, large home sits between a vacant lot and a twin-sized house accommodating the offices of the Performing Arts Training Center. Six stone steps lead up to the house from the curb, followed by the house's own separate set of four steps, which lead to its entrance inside a small enclosed porch. Dunham's home reflects her own good taste and warmth. Imported furniture and artifacts, healthy, green, and evidently well-tended plants are everywhere, giving the house style. In the living room, off to one corner, an easel always stands upright with the current oil painting left unfinished. The easel is left standing so that, during any rare free time, she can pick up a random brush and add a few more colorful strokes. In the rear of the house, the kitchen is completely modern and is always filled with exquisite aromas of good things cooking. Her favorite color, navy, is even made evident in her choice of navy and white patterned dishes.

This setting *seems* quite normal, yet why are folks reluctant to visit her home? The reason was finally revealed to her one day when she talked to some members of the community about where to hold a meeting, and said, "All right, let's have the meeting over at *our* place in the conference hall; it's pleasant and it's large."

One member answered, "Well, I just think we'd better have it on the main campus or someplace else."

Dunham didn't feel that this remark was directed against her because she was a key member of the particular meeting. Later, she was questioning her staff about the incident when someone remarked, "Well, you know, they are afraid to come here because you practice black magic; when they see that black Virgin, they are frightened."

At the peak of the black awareness movement of the sixties when people did visit her home on Tenth Street and saw her black Virgin, they would be startled. To Dunham, their reaction was always strange. Why, in the midst of the black power struggle, would people feel threatened by a black Virgin? Since they accepted all the white spiritual figures in church, such as the Virgin Mary and Christ, their refusal to accept a black spiritual figure was a mystery to her. The Cubans, for instance, have always had black Virgins; some Spanish Virgins are also black, such as the Spanish protector of bullfighters, the Macarena, Virgin of Guadelupe.

Where is this black Virgin in her home? From the entrance hallway, stairs lead up to the second floor. On the landing of the stairway, just where it curves to continue upward, a small altar holds the black Virgin of Regla, Yemanja, Dunham's Goddess in both Cuba and Brazil. Yemanja (Cuban, De la Regla) is ceramic and wears the usual vestments worn by a Christian Virgin. The ceramic Yemanja in fact resembles a Virgin Mary statue, except that her skin is brown and her hair black. Yemanja is draped in blue and white and wears small beads that are the color of the sea. On the altar a candle always burns.

The black Virgin is surrounded by the other virgins and saints that Dunham serves. Legba (Cuban, Alegba) is the guardian of gates and crossroads. Similar to the Christian St. Peter, the gatekeeper, Legba is called upon to open the gates to permit spirits of other gods to penetrate the souls of worshippers. No *vaudun* service can begin in earnest without Legba's permission. Legba's *vévé*, an intricate corn-meal *vaudun* design, sometimes inscribed by the *houngan* around the *poteau-mitan*, or central post of the *tonnelle*, is similar to a very lacy wrought-iron gate. Legba has miniature toys such as tops, whistles, and marbles placed around him as well as miniature weapons such as guns and knives, and a ladder to climb out of difficulties. On a chain bracelet are warriors' tools such as pliers, scissors, a saw, and a hammer. Legba is draped with beads of red and black, his traditional colors.

Ochun, goddess of the river (Cuban, De la Cobre), wears yellow beads.

St. Lazarus (Cuban, San Lazaro), the saint for crippled joints, is served by Dunham because of her injured knees. This saint carries crutches and has sores on his body. Two dogs sit at the base of the statue to lick his visible wounds. St. Lazaros wears two strings of beads—one is intermingled blue and white, the other is multicolored.

Her dear friend and priestess, Godmother Rosita, who lives in Miami, told her that she must keep an altar to Yemanja and taught her how to care for it. Expressing her particular belief in what gods of African origin can do, Dunham says that many people are alive today in one place or another because of Rosita's intervention as middleperson between the worshipper and the god.

Through her interest in the priesthoods of Cuba and Brazil and her ever-growing knowledge of Haitian *vaudun*, Dunham thinks Rosita sums it up accurately when she says, "You are a legitimate daughter of Yemanja in four ways." After her godmother had cast her shells four times, the answer appeared that Dunham was not an adopted daughter, who only offers as a servant to Yemanja, but a legitimate daughter who prayed and listened to hear. Therefore, Yemanja has an obligation toward Dunham over and beyond that she owes an ordinary person. In return, Dunham has obligations she must meet to appease and show gratitude to the virgin.

The first step of her *vaudun* initiation, referred to as *lavé tête,* took place during her early research in Haiti in the late thirties and was arranged by Dunham's long-time friends, Doc Reeser and Fred Allsop. The preparations for the *lavé tête* initiation took months. Special lotions, scented waters, liquors, cornmeal, oil, seasonings, and the proper clothing had to be secured. Although no specific price tag is connected with an initiation, the initiate must supply all requests for appeasement according to the demands of a particular *loa*, or spirit. The basic clothing, which must be purchased by all *hounci lavé tête* candidates in the Arada–Dahomey cult, is a new, white, cambric sleeping gown and a second new outfit in the colors of the chosen *loa*. The initiation, which takes place in a remote section of the village in a *peristyle* (or sacred place), starts by chanting and offering prayers to Legba. Sacred food that pleases the *loa*, which must be of finest quality, is then offered. Knowing of the great Haitian god Damballa's love of fowl, Dunham offered two plump, white roosters along with other gifts consisting of ointments, jewelry, liqueurs, holy pictures, cologne, cornmeal, and eggs. If at any time the *loa* speaks through the possessed representative and asks for a last-minute gift the *hounci* initiate cannot produce, a promissary note is signed and accepted. Fortunately, Dunham's offerings were sufficient.

As Africans emigrated to Haiti, they kept their gods. Dunham was told that Damballa, represented by the serpent and the rainbow, was her special god. Damballa is married to Aïda Quedo, the virgin mother. Erzulie is the name given his mistress. Together, Damballa and Aïda inhabit the sky and control the universe. From their position representing married authority, other gods of lesser powers have branched off, such as Legba, Shango, and Agwe. At each initiation, Damballa chooses one of his newly initiated to "marry." In the course of the *lavé tête* ritual, Damballa "mounts" or chooses an initiate. Dunham was thus selected as Damballa's bride. Like a husband or lover, Damballa is jealous. Since her marriage to Damballa, she has had the burden of punishment if his demands are not met for any need of jealousy on his part. According to Haitian belief, one cannot divorce Damballa; in that respect the *vaudun* and Catholic religions are similar.

For the initiation, Dunham, along with eight other initiates, was placed on her side on the dirt floor of a *houngfor,* or temple, in such a fashion that each one snugly touched the person in front. They were then instructed to bend their knees, thus causing the initiate in front to have a mock lap to sit on. They all remained in this soon-to-become-painful position until instructed by the priestess to "rise up and turn." This command was given every few hours. After carrying out the order, the group settled into the same position on the other side.

The priestess then checked each initiate several times to see if a *loa* was about to be presented or had entered his body. Dunham wondered what signs or movements led a priest to declare that a *loa* had entered a *hounci.* Was it a facial expression? A movement of the body? What? She decided it was one of the many magical mysteries inherent in being a *houngan* or priestess.

The priestess then passed among them and touched their heads which had been bound in white cloth. Under the cloth, offerings to their particular *loa* were placed. Damballa, Dunham's *loa*, required that her hair be matted with cornmeal, feathers, *orgeat*—a syrupy drink with an almond liquid base—chicken, blood, herbs, and raw eggs. Sometimes cooked sacrificial food was added to her already overloaded hair. The head was to stay wrapped for the entire length of the ritual, three days. One can imagine the discomfort and odor of the offering combined with the odor of sweat from the heat, which by the end of the ritual seemed unbearable.

For one week after the initiation or "arising," the initiates continued to wear the sacrificial headwrap. Their heads also remained bound with baptismal kerchiefs. Because she didn't want to be questioned, Dunham wore a blue headkerchief over which she sometimes placed a straw hat to conceal the ingredients.

Then Dunham returned to the village for the removal of her headdress. There was no ceremony in this act. A helper, who assisted her in removing the ceremonial objects, kept what she could from the tangled and matted roots for use in the *pot tête*, a covered china pot in which the *loa* and spirits are kept, placed in one's living quarters. Small remnants of personal baptismal sacrifices placed in *pot têtes* are considered to contain the *mana* or spiritual essence of the owner. The hair that came out in the comb was then given to her and tied in a cloth. Dunham felt a great relief when the bizarre head-dress could be removed and her hair washed clean.

Many people of primitive faiths are convinced that an enemy can cause migrains and other ailments of the head by obtaining a strand of hair. Thus, natives protect the valuable and ornate hair containers on their dresser tops which are ready for the immediate deposit of their combed-out hair. This hair is then disposed of or burned to ward off evil spells, which would be cast by the enemy.

A *hounci canzo*, a servitor of the gods who has been tamed or controlled, can be of either sex. In the fire ritual, the *hounci*, during a hypnotic state called "possession," is capable of extreme exposure to heat without showing visible signs of injury. For this ritual Dunham held a big ceremony at her estate, Habitation Leclerc, in 1974. Although she passed the ritual, her final requirement before becoming a full-fledged *mambo* is to learn the secret of the *ason*, the sacred gourd rattle that is surrounded by snake vertebra and which is only used by the *houngan* or *mambo*, priest or priestess.*

Thus, her decision to be a *hounci* initiate, a server of the *vaudun*

---

*At present, Dunham is completing the intricate training process required to become a *mambo*.

cults of Haiti, Brazil, and Cuba, was the first religious choice she had made.

Dunham knows that many people with primitive faiths live in pockets in the interior of the Caribbean, South America, and even North America. They have had their culture uninterrupted by colonialism since the time of slavery. She is still fascinated by the very private ceremonies of Haiti, many of which use no drums, but evoke the gods by means of sacred objects, songs, and the recitations of holy litanies and prayers.

In today's more tolerant society, the private Haitian home ceremonies have recently been able to "come out of the closet." Small shops, visible in sophisticated cities in the United States, cater to the occult, as their store-front signs clearly state. Young people, some of whom have turned away from more formal and acceptable religions, have begun to seek new ways to express their needs and beliefs through primitive religions.

For Haitian ceremonies, villagers bring all sorts of odds and ends for sacrifices. There are *gris-gris*, sacks on a cord tied around the neck which can be worn in clear view or hidden to guard against ill health or loss of property; and *oungas*, or charms, that are often bound with yards and yards of wire and are hung in various places on the property or buried. For negative or positive control, there are love potions and powders. Sometimes, various parts of a sacrificial goat or chicken may be powdered or soaked, or ground up and placed in the *ounga* charm so that someone can either be summoned to them or be put to shame. Other charms may contain pounded snake vertebra or, since Haiti is known for its rich plant and herbal life, all sorts of plants and herbs. The Arawak and Carib indians, who were in Haiti before the Africans, were experienced herbalists.

Charms are never purchased in fully assembled form. The priest or priestess may use twenty or thirty items before being satisfied with the particular charm's potency. Often Dunham was told to wait for a period of several days to secure a more specific ingredient from the "pharmacy." She has visited some of these cult pharmacies, not only in the Caribbean, but in neighborhoods in New York. They also exist in the Far East, South America, and Africa.

Haitian pharmacies are often tiny wooden stores. The eight-foot-tall lavaliere doors fold open, as if to invite one inside a doll-sized drug and herb store. The shelves are packed to the ceiling with jars and bottles. On one side, prepared commercial stock is kept. This merchandise is often American with its trade name translated into French. To a novice American shopper who doesn't read French, the familiar logo of a brand is its only recognizable sign. These bottles are often dust covered, letting you know that their contents, due to the lack of demand, are probably too old to be effective. On the opposite wall in the enclosed counter display cases are the more popular Haitian folk medicines whose bottles are shiny, new, and dust free. Immediately one knows the Haitians' shopping preferences.

Dunham's belief in the power of some of these *gris-gris* and *oungas* is shown by the fact that several different-shaped pots and jars stay on her altar. One such "protector," a small, furry, brown, stuffed toy monkey, is about six inches tall. It hangs in her sleeping quarters and is always present whether she is in California or Haiti.

Every New Year's Eve, Rosita gives Dunham specific instructions to insure her of a healthy and prosperous year. Once she was instructed to cover the entire floor in every room with popcorn to appease the Haitian gods. The new year thus began energetically with the sweeping of all of the leftover popcorn out of the house New Year's Day. On an equally colorful New Year's Eve, 1975, Cero, my husband, and I were visiting Dunham, her family, and her friends at her villa in Haiti. Just before midnight Dunham, dressed in white, entered each suite and swung incense encased in an ornate brass ball on a long chain into every room to purify it. This ritual was followed by a glorious feast.

They say that black cats are the pets of witches. Conversely, Dunham's cat in Haiti, Yam, is large and white with only a spot or two of black. Yam is most often seen with her mistress, and it is Dunham's belief that cats are Cancerian, like herself, and although homebodies, also like to remain slightly aloof. Her cat Thai that died recently in East St. Louis was large and gray with yellow eyes that sometimes changed to green. Thai certainly fortified the gossip about Dunham's witchery, since he thought himself a person. Because

Dunham felt it would be cruel to force a cat to travel, knowing it was a cat's nature to be in familiar surroundings, she never took Thai along on business trips.

Residents of East St. Louis might also have heard the legend that Habitation Leclerc was haunted. In truth, Dunham has had Kam, her godmother in Haiti, exorcise spirits of past slaves that were killed and buried on the property. Annette Dunham, her mother, was visiting her at the time and had no prior knowledge of the legend. One night Annette became hysterical when she swore a thief had come to her bedroom. The puzzling part of the incident was that the thief had had both hands bound behind his back and, after she screamed, had fled toward the old deserted slave quarters. Kam also exorcised an apparition of a thin, pale woman who wore a white, flowing gown and jewels and who was believed to have been Pauline Bonaparte. The woman was often seen at night around the private pool Pauline had once been known to frequent. After three days of successful meditation and communication with Lenguesou, a *vaudun* god, Kam caused the feeling of evil to leave. This was only one among many exorcisms done to completely free Leclerc of evil spirits.

As for orthodox Christian beliefs, Dunham has never been baptized or christened. Although she attended the African Methodist Episcopal Church in Joliet, Illinois during her adolescence, her parents overlooked the official aspect of having her christened or baptized. Therefore, when viewing it from the standpoint of a lay person, Dunham probably feels she *is* a witch.

Often people ask Dunham if she thinks they should become initiates. She is frequently suspicious of their intentions, feeling they seek initiation as an escape or a dependent way of life. Still, she attempts to explain to them the seriousness of the step.

The fact that some still consider her a sorceress no longer troubles her. She chooses to remain animistic, knowing that she has seen in these ceremonies of spirits happenings that would be called miracles in more conventional churches. These experiences and her continuing communication with a *vaudun* high priest and priestess satisfy Dunham—she is certain that her gods protect her. Quite simply, she only wishes for a continued creative and productive life. To make certain she will get her wish, she knocks on wood.

Frequently the very people in her East St. Louis community who believe she is a witch and ridicule her are those who seek her out, requesting advice and counsel. She considers this paradox amusing. For the most part these visitors follow the same pattern. They never come in the daytime, but as soon as darkness will shield them, they make their move, nearly always alone. The bell rings and a very nervous visitor enters. After being greeted cordially, his or her tension mounts. There is always a stab at small talk: "How are the classes going? How is your health? How are the senior citizens' classes?"—all questions to make the visit seem like a casual house call. Usually Dunham goes along with the game, waiting patiently to see what approach the person will use to explain the real reason for the visit. Would help perhaps be needed in some personal, financial, or family problem? After much hemming and hawing, the visitor nearly always swallows pride and asks questions such as: "Is it true my husband has a lover?" "Will I get a job?" "Should I move my family out West?" Knowing the courage it has probably taken to come to her house on Tenth Street with its altar to the black Virgin, Dunham never takes such pleas lightly. She will genuinely seek help for the visitor. In the event that she is not able to counsel and guide the person to her satisfaction, she will send their name to Rosita, asking the godmother to consult her cowrie shells and her gods. In return, Rosita will send her what help she can.

Rosita always asks Dunham why she worries. Being a legitimate daughter of Yemanja and wife of Damballa, she shouldn't be disturbed if things don't go the way she wants. If Yemanja, the Virgin, is rightly served, she will always see to it that problems are solved. Just as people offer Christian prayers, Dunham asks of Yemanja, "Look, I'm your legitimate daughter—you owe me this. Now see to it." Her requests to Yemanja have for her the same benefits as prayers for people who pray.

Dunham relates an interesting story of a young East St. Louis militant. The principal aim of Dunham's work with various East St. Louis street gangs was to help them take a more realistic look at their life-style in the ghetto since it formed a basis for their fight against racism. As a result, a trust existed between her and various gang members. Frequently they visited her home on North Tenth Street for guidance. One night while Rosita was visiting, a young man in great trouble stopped by. The man's only exposure to religion had been through conventional Protestantism. He found Rosita's drama of casting shells, followed by chants and other rituals, completely foreign. Nevertheless, knowing his life was at a very low point, he was willing to try anything to improve it. Rosita told him he would be fine if he turned over his future to her protection. Rosita sensed in him qualities for being a *santero* or priest—a member of a Cuban *Lucumi* cult. Usually it takes two to seven years and thousands of dollars to become a full-fledged *santero*, but with the eye of a psychologist Rosita immediately recognized his leadership and strength. Priests and priestesses are very sensitive to human behavior. Since visiting North Tenth Street and meeting Rosita, the young man has become an important figure in the politics of East St. Louis.

East St. Louis

An excerpt from "Observations: East St. Louis, Illinois" by Katherine Dunham.

Here in East St. Louis
We're hungry
And don't know it. . . .
The hopeless shapeless feeling
Of an unidentified pain.

I know how to say
Motha-fuggah
How to throw down rot-gut
From a bottle labeled "whiskey."
How to Boogaloo and Funky Butt.
Talk about a flat-back ho'
Without money for two minutes in the bed of one
Unless she gives it to me.

I call my Brothers Niggah and Tombstone
Candy, Coon, and Dog,
Without ever knowing where they live
Or if they have another name. . . .
Small and large
Those who dream,
Those who lean on the thin edge

East St. Louis

Of reality
Waking long enough to retch
Or vomit food that isn't there,
We stay in the street,
A "junk" shop,
In a bar;
Bum a ride in someone's
Antiquated car
To go—where?
From 15th to 26th to Bond to Broadway
Maybe State, Missouri and on rare occasions
Cross the bridge
To Pruitt–Igoe for a ball
That may end up a brawl
That may end up in jail
Without bail. . . .

Sometimes I come to life.
A new beat from a Congo drum
A new record in the juke box if it's right.
A stranger come to town,
An hour with Rap Brown,
A brother shot and killed for right or wrong.
Then back again to concentrate
On Nothing.

The third chronological period in Katherine Dunham's life,
which she refers to as her period of "personal education," was
spent in East St. Louis. The ramifications of this period are great
in terms of their influence on further research she has undertaken,
not only in the United States, but in South America, Africa, and
Haiti. As director of the Performing Arts Training Center (PATC) at
Southern Illinois University, she daily experiences the challenges,
conflicts, and successes that face contemporary black youth. She is
concerned not only with their high rate of illiteracy, but also with
the fact that many drop out of school before the age of sixteen. With
the PATC, her main hope is that, through changing their environ-
ment, she can change their attitude toward learning.

The maternal feeling she exhibits toward East St. Louis is natural, for Dunham has a kind, rare sympathy for people. This emotional investment is always present. Reflecting on the days of her research in the Caribbean, she can recall being personally involved with the poor people of the villages. In Haiti, whenever she left a village there would always be some old or young person who would cry, and she would cry, too. Dunham is often considered authoritarian; yet, whenever she is involved with people it is done with all the depth that her person and personality can give. One example of this is her work with senior citizens in East St. Louis.

Dunham is very concerned not only with the devastating financial circumstances in which senior citizens live in affluent America, but also with the poor quality of cultural and recreational facilities available to them. Recently she started a branch of Senior Citizens for the Performing Arts that enables seniors to regularly attend plays and other cultural events. In addition, they work with trained young people who aid and assist them with body movement and conditioning. These special senior students learn physical fitness, as well as square and ring dances. In 1970 they even toured as far as Providence, Rhode Island to give lecture demonstrations to show off their skills and educate others of their age on the value of the movements. To East St. Louis seniors the tour was exciting and the experience of traveling added a new dimension to their lives. In response to her friend Erich Fromm's statement that "All art is humanistic," Dunham, taking it a step further, says, "All artists are humanists."

PATC is a two-year school located in the old Broadview Hotel on Pennsylvania and Broadway. The seventh floor has a new, large, bright, mirrored studio which also houses audio and visual equipment. The ground floor has a smaller studio where children's classes are held.

The courses offered are
Performing Arts
        Dance, drama, music, martial arts.

Applied Skills
> African hair braiding, African wood carving, visual arts, visual design, commercial design, pattern making, and theater crafts.

Humanities
> Languages (conversation stressed more than grammar), aesthetics, social sciences, African nations today, African government, and various theater courses. (In the humanities division, the educational philosophy focuses on teaching students how to deal with their own community before branching out to cope with the world at large.)

Dunham had two assignments at Southern Illinois University before beginning her work at PATC in 1967. She was artist-in-residence at the Carbondale campus in the Fine Arts Department in 1965; then she was the choreographer, stage director, and assistant director to Marjorie Lawrence for the opera *Faust*. Dunham placed it in a World War II German setting, implying a comparison to Hitler. Later she found that, due to her innovative approach with the opera, President Delyte Morris had stated, "she must stay or come back." She stayed three months longer, and in 1967 returned for good.

During her artist-in-residency her archives had been established on the Carbondale campus. In the SIU complex there are four campuses: Carbondale, Alton, Edwardsville, and East St. Louis. Edwardsville is PATC's "mother" campus. Everyone agreed that there was almost too much material to be housed solely at Carbondale, for contained in the archives were costumes, original manuscripts, artifacts, personel correspondence, photos, and literary works. Fortunately the university has taken meticulous care of the material, making most of it readily accessible to the public. Upon Dunham's request some personal correspondence cannot be opened until after her death. Similarly, miscellaneous material (such as costumes, objects, and odds-and-ends), in which people would see no value unless they were assembled in the way an archeologist pieces together his findings, are at the Katherine Dunham Museum in East St. Louis. If it hadn't been for SIU President Morris' insistence that

East St. Louis *needed* a massive input of cultural opportunity, much of her material might have been stored in SIU's mother campus in Edwardsville, twenty miles away. Morris felt that the people of East St. Louis had to be informed of their rich cultural background. For example, Miles Davis, the jazz trumpeter, and Josephine Baker, the international singing star, were born there. For years the East St. Louis jazz sound was heard the world over. Even the great Edward Kennedy "Duke" Ellington's band praised it in the song "East St. Louis Toodle-oo" made popular in the thirties. Before his retirement, Morris recognized this great heritage and voiced hopes of making East St. Louis a vast midwestern cultural center deriving in part from Dunham's efforts.

The basic support of the original museum, established in 1968 at 460 North Ninth Street in the basement of the PATC complex, had been supplied by the university. But when the PATC first decided to move from its original location on Ninth Street to its present home on Broadway and Pennsylvania, no space was available, which resulted in the museum's closing down temporarily.

In 1969 Dunham presented a proposal to the Chamber of Commerce to reopen the Dynamic Museum, established the year before but which could not be moved to the new quarters due to lack of space and had to be closed. The Chamber of Commerce was responsive to the idea and decided to revive the museum in a new and different manner. Instead of a large exposition hall, which the previous museum had had, it recommended that a number of small rooms for displaying rare objects and a work and storage room with a revolving display be substituted.

The new Katherine Dunham Museum, which opened in late 1977, now houses artifacts of her personal life and the life of the Dunham Company. It is located at 1005 Pennsylvania in a building constructed in 1894. The large, brick, mansion-type structure sits on a massive corner lot that includes a large parking area. An old, stately carriage house is in the rear. The newly opened space houses not only the Katherine Dunham Museum, but also the Institute for Intercultural Communication as well as a gallery of African art objects obtained from Dunham's collection and that of Jeanelle Stovall, her colleague, who had gathered them while living in Africa.

Other friends' pieces are also on display. Dunham finds it gratifying to see people from all walks of life touring the museum to look at the collection.

Dunham believes that every community, no matter where it is located, should have a display of visual art that is indigenous and of historical value. One of her hopes is to one day present an exhibit based on the art of Appalachians and blacks from the area. The East St. Louis community, she feels, should draw from these areas of their own wealth, thus making both students and visitors aware of this rich source of midwestern culture.

In the beginning of the PATC, during the hot summers of the race riots of the sixties, every day proved to be a lesson in self-discipline and control. Several times during this period Dunham's life was threatened because she spent so much time with militant young adults. She knew they couldn't possibly win on the course they were following, and would probably end up dead. Nevertheless, she worked with them patiently in an attempt to instill in their minds new values through a thorough training in martial and performing arts. Once, some university officials telephoned to say, "We have been told that it's best for you to leave town."

"I'm not going to leave town," was her answer.

"Well, you're there at your own risk."

"That's perfectly all right with me."

Again, the officials cautioned, "There's been an actual threat on your life if you don't stop circulating among these people."

Impact House was the name of the place where the militants held their meetings. The officials ordered Dunham to stay away. Although she'd never visited the clubhouse, upon hearing the order she obstinately decided to go there. She knew she had to see for herself what was going on. Impact House was a run-down building with old chairs and tables of assorted vintage placed around the sides of a large meeting room. It was the central place for planning survival strategy at a time when even "survival" seemed futile. Entering the house with courage she didn't know she possessed, Dunham presented a proposal to a group of the most feared young people in East St. Louis, a gang called "the Warlords." When she entered, the members regarded with hostility the sight of a stately, well-dressed black woman who had dared enter their private domain. Courageously she stood her ground. She then presented a unique proposal that offered the street men courses at PATC in martial arts, congo drumming, and dance. The most active militants, the young Warlords, would go to dance classes; the older Warlords, in their teens, would observe the dance, but only participate in karate and drumming. Immediately they sensed her honesty and genuine desire to help. Also they admired and respected her fearless entrance to their clubhouse, knowing full well that the average citizen would never dare tread across their doorstep. Dunham's courage began a rapport that eventually led to her being given protection by the gang members.

In East St. Louis, Dunham often walked with young people whose names were on police cards, allegedly with instructions that they should be shot on sight. She would invite these militants to accompany her on various school and city matters. Together they walked the dangerous streets while police cars circled the blocks during the entire course of their journey. They consciously ignored the police harassment.

Once Jeanelle and Dunham were told in confidence that their buildings were to be bombed. So many buildings had been bombed that Dunham was surprised PATC hadn't been chosen as a target long before. Pausing to knock on wood, a gesture she always makes, Dunham prepared for the worst. Although PATC was spared, the bombings continued. Dunham always grew frightened when she heard sirens or looked out of her windows and saw fires blazing around her so close she could actually smell them. An emergency phone network, set up by the community so news could be sent in a very short time to anyone listed within the network area, informed her what was happening during the bombings. Sometimes snipers would shoot. Unfortunately, the buildings were easy targets both for bombings and sniper attacks by whites from the surrounding small towns. Sleeping in them was therefore dangerous. Finally, Dunham became conditioned. Her tension reached the point that, although asleep, whenever she heard an unexpected sound or sensed anything the least bit unusual, she would awaken, expecting an explosion.

It took her time to realize that her personal mission with the

East St. Louis community would not be accomplished immediately. Nevertheless, looking at her mission today with maturity and objectivity, she sees that a great deal has been done. She doesn't have to resort to innumerable press clippings, reviews by critics, or observations of social scientists to know that the very "soul" of East St. Louis has been influenced by PATC.

In the beginning of her work at PATC she did not want the pressures of a professional company. Nevertheless, she realized that as students became advanced they would need a performing outlet. During the early months of classes she observed a group of talented young people that were advancing in their skills to the extent that a mini-company could be formed. Dunham immediately began to reconstruct some of her pieces on the new group with great results.

In 1968, the student company performed throughout Illinois, from Cairo to Chicago, before more than 500,000 spectators. They even traveled as far as Connecticut, Rhode Island, Missouri, Ohio, Washington, D.C., and Jacksonville, Florida doing benefit performances with no set fee other than expenses that would cover twenty-five to thirty performers and crew. Whatever donations they received were put into the PATC fund to assist with future productions. Dunham made it very clear that the company was not the "Dunham Company," but representatives of the East St. Louis PATC. Dunham feels that exposure through travel to people from other areas is a very vital part of a student's growth; therefore she is always seeking funds with which this can be accomplished. Her philosophy is that travel enriches people, especially when their social experience has been limited to an isolated area.

Not only has the experience of performing saved many young people from a future of crime and violence but, for many adults in East St. Louis, PATC has meant a new experience both in growth and in hope.

The staff is underwritten by the university. Any guest teachers or consultants must be paid by other sources. Her present master teachers are former members of her company and include Archie Savage from her original company and Tommy Gomez, Lenwood Morris, and Norman Walter Davis. They conduct classes and instruct student teachers in Dunham technique to ensure its preservation.

Although Dunham has been accused of not being willing to fire any instructors, it is hard for her to discharge anyone in East St. Louis. She knows their side of it too well. Consequently, she has a problem with chiefs-of-staff who occasionally say that such-and-such person *must* go, or that, since they're not good for a particular problem, they should be fired. Even if Dunham agrees, she'll immediately begin to sift out the person's good points or even invent some to keep them. Presently this is her major administrative difficulty. Sometimes she has kept instructors who have improved and changed. It is typical of a Cancerian, her astrological sign, to have almost blind loyalty. Should someone be completely destructive, she can quickly do away with their association; yet when she knows they have tried their best, she is extremely tolerant. At other times she is pleased when instructors reach a professional level that enables them to leave on their own without difficulty or embarrassment.

Her first hope for students is that they develop some sort of tie to East St. Louis. Hopefully they can fulfill the current need for performing artists and teachers in the city's local school system, thereby enriching an area that is at present socially and economically deprived. If they do not choose to remain, she hopes they will join a major dance company. Admittedly, she is reluctant to see star pupils leave—naturally she would like to see them stay to build East St. Louis. Nevertheless, she has learned from earlier experience that there comes a time when some students must venture out on their own.

Various dance companies, when passing through the area, look forward to the opportunity of studying Dunham technique from its source. They always leave PATC with a new respect for the technique and its creator, Katherine Dunham.

Although Dunham did not feel that the Chamber of Commerce was racially prejudiced, she knew it alone had the power to set up the future course of the city both by deciding what industry existed and by bringing jobs and deciding what big business contracts were signed in Washington. Giving the Chamber the benefit of the doubt, Dunham decided that it had not yet found a group of blacks who could operate on behalf of the city instead of their own personal gain. Once during a meeting of the Chamber, Dunham stated, "This is an inanimate city, a city lacking in its thinking and in so many of its different facets. Businesses, banks, water, electricity, and land reclamations are all controlled by white people."

Dunham and her assistant director Jeanelle Stovall were both disturbed over what they had observed at this particular meeting. After working hours, East St. Louis is ninety to ninety-five percent black. Practically all members of the Chamber of Commerce lived outside the city and at the close of the work day headed for outlying "bedroom" communities. At meetings such as these, she and Jeanelle were frequently the only black guests present, a fact that weighed heavily on their minds.

Repeatedly Dunham asked herself, "Why are no more black members present?" Since the town's mayor was black, she couldn't continually blame limited attendance of blacks on the Chamber of Commerce itself or on white people. Analyzing the situation, she decided that East St. Louis blacks as a people were unprepared. Although they belonged in small numbers to the Chamber, they seldom attended meetings to cast their vote on needed issues. A certain business sense or academic preparation seemed needed in order to cope with local and national political problems. Also, it took a great wealth of experience coupled with serious industrial know-how to represent concerns such as the city water works or gas and electricity services.

In spite of her frustration over the apathy of East St. Louis blacks, Dunham courageously challenged the Chamber to be more aware of its obligation to its black community. In proposing that the St. Louis Cultural Center be established in East St. Louis, Dunham wanted blacks to support her bid. She didn't think a white Chamber of Commerce could have total responsibility over the future location of a cultural center. Furthermore, former Southern Illinois University President Morris shared her viewpoint.

Taking seriously the cliché that the most important black business is in funeral parlors, Dunham approached Marion Officer, a mortician, whom she considered more financially solvent than various white men at the meeting with whom she had spoken. Along with other blacks who represented the civic and financial interests of the city, Marion was conspicuously absent from meetings she attended. The mayor already had to cope with a two-thirds majority white council inherited from an earlier administration and built-in corruption influenced by the Chicago political machine. So she felt the black population had a responsibility to give their full support by attending meetings "on time" and without carrying "a chip on their shoulder." A desire to see East St. Louis progress should be every black citizen's goal. She asked Marion, "What *is* East St. Louis? Doesn't it mean anything to blacks to have an exciting, progressive community, with a hope for its future being run by blacks?"*

During the 1973 mayoral election, some gossiped that Dunham wanted to run for mayor. It was suspected that was why she was launching PATC. It was said that she was after personal backing from the Illinois governor. Since she had recently been decorated by him with the Lincoln Academy Award, some felt PATC had been organized for her political advancement. Dunham realizes that many believe she is using both city and university for personal gain, but ignores this criticism and continues to serve on state and local boards when asked. During the mid-sixties race riots, she often phoned Springfield and sent telegrams to other state governors and even congressmen and senators in Washington to aid young militants caught in the plight of false imprisonment. When state troopers arrived intent on suppressing riots in the schools, she continually voiced her protest to politicians. If her actions gave the impression of extreme self-interest, she paid no attention.

Dunham was born in the Midwest and educated in anthropology; she was exposed to the world of ideas during her period of touring in Africa and the West Indies. Without this background she feels that she could not have come to East St. Louis and stayed, successfully witnessing the development of PATC.

Dunham believes that it's harder to be a woman in the Midwest than in any other area in America. More sexual discrimination than racial discrimination is present since the Midwest is essentially conservative and upholds the traditional stereotype of what a

---

*Marion Officer's son, Carl Officer, has just won the Mayoral election at the age of 26 and promises to rid the city of its often-St. Louis-dominated corruption.

woman's role should be. Dunham hopes the stance taken by the women's liberation movement will help the Midwestern woman. For Dunham it has been difficult to be a woman director, a position of responsibility with social status equal to that of a university professor. (She herself is an accredited professor.) It is difficult not only because she came to East St. Louis after having starred in her own company where she was sole authority for many years, but also because she has had the respect of chiefs-of-state and never has had her authority challenged. In her attempts to institute vital programs for the survival of blacks in East St. Louis she is constantly challenged. She says, "If East St. Louis survives, it will be an indication of the strength of the black race, and of the civilization of the white race."

True, False, and Other Myths
A Conversation with Katherine Dunham

During one of our many sessions together in the planning stages of this book, Miss D and I began to reminisce about rumors. Rumors that often accompany an artist of her calibre are plentiful and are often never cleared up by the star. Usually the press and the public only take in the initial sensationalism or gossip. I told Miss D that this is her opportunity to "set the record straight."

Q. Let's take it from the top and see what happens.
A. Well, I will do my best. Today there's still a lot of controversy among company members as to whether *this* was true or *that* was true. Lenwood Morris, whom we all say has a memory like an elephant, will sometimes come up with things about which I'm completely left in a daze. I can't remember some of these things happening, yet I'll do my best.

Q. Do you have a sense of humor?
A. I think I do. I *know* I do. Sometimes I'll say "with my perverted sense of humor" and then make a statement, but I think I have a sense of humor which is, well, I'd like to think *sophisticated*. Frequently it's very dry, and sometimes quite roundabout, but if I didn't find so much in life amusing, I don't think I really could have supported the things that have been difficult in this long career. My answer is yes. I think I have a great sense of humor, but I think it's very special and hard to get at.

Q. Did Aly Kahn give you a diamond necklace?

A. Oh, this rumor will never go to its grave. Aly Kahn did *not* give me a diamond necklace. He gave me nothing more than some pleasant evenings. I met him through a friend of mine, Doris Duke, and we would sometimes go dancing. He loved to dance. At that time I would often leave the theater to go out in Paris to clubs, etc. I found Aly a charming person, very pleasant and good company. But beyond this, absolutely "zero" on rumors.

The famous diamond necklace was bought by *me*. A jeweler in Paris whose name was Sterle saw our show. He was a man who was very creative and showed extremely good taste in his work; so when he came to me with a drawing and a plan of what he thought I should wear—a very simple necklace of baguette diamonds with a pear drop—I had to have it. Yet I couldn't afford it. As a matter of fact, I did many things in Paris that I couldn't afford as a result of being taken in by the city and its great designers, couturiers, jewelers, etc. My heart was set on this necklace which my husband also helped persuade me to buy. So eventually, after a long period of gathering funds together and making time payments, I owned it. That's the truth of it. I don't know how this rumor, which made headlines in various newspapers, began.

Q. Were you ever embarrassed by company members' failures?

A. Let me back up on the Aly Kahn situation before I answer that. It was also rumored and even printed, to my great embarrassment, that I was carrying on in such a way with Aly that Rita Hayworth, his wife, was going to name me in a divorce suit. Now that was absolute absurdity. When I saw Miss Hayworth, our company was appearing at Ciro's in Hollywood. I had met her once before and we spoke most cordially. I knew then that she really didn't believe the rumor. Somebody had made it up to make a cheap and flashy headline.

Q. Company members' failings—were you embarrassed by them?

A. Sometimes. I remember a girl who traveled with us from Chicago. It was the first trip out of Chicago for most of the young people in the company. This girl was very, should I say, prissy and pompous, if you get the picture, so much so that she had changed her name four times during her life, seeking some identity other than American black. We got in the Pullman diner on the train. We were on our way somewhere, maybe it was on the way West, I don't know. I was sitting at another table and I noticed the waiter becoming more and more exasperated. This was unusual because as you know, all Pullman car porters and waiters were black as a result of a regulation left many years ago by old man Pullman; so it was always a relief to us to know we could at least go to the dining car and not have problems. But this waiter was getting exasperated, so I thought, "What's wrong?" and began to watch. This young lady had ordered scrambled whites of eggs. I think the waiter just blocked out the whites and brought scrambled eggs. Well, she wasn't satisfied and they were returned. The waiter was really upset. He finally had brought her some plain eggs up-right. If she wanted only the whites, she could pick them out and eat them. This didn't happen, and the plate went back again. The young lady became indignant and said, "I don't eat *anything* but the scrambled whites of eggs." I think she ended up not getting breakfast. I think that the waiter was thoroughly disgusted, and I was embarrassed.

And then, on a number of occasions I have become embarrassed by things which probably shouldn't have disturbed me. In our first ballet choreographed by Ruth Page in the early thirties in which I first appeared at the Chicago Opera, I was in charge of a large body of the corps de ballet. The ballet was set in Martinique. At that time I had not yet been to the West Indies, but I had the leading part. I also assisted Ruth Page with the choreography.

We selected young people for the corps from Chicago's South Side. Most had probably never heard of ballet. Today they were what would be called "inner-city" young people. They were given choice dressing rooms. At the end of the show on my way out, I noticed that in most rooms the drawers had been pulled out of most of the dressing tables. There was great disorder, showers had been left running—I was wild, to say the least. I think there was comment afterward that the ballet's next appearance during the season would be cancelled because of the behavior of the corps of this particular ballet. I was extremely embarrassed by it. Now and in later years I would accept the situation as it is—that people who are unaccustomed to something often react leaving a mark of almost ecstatic delirium.

Q. Did Sol Hurok insure your legs for a million dollars?

A. Well, that was the story. Sol Hurok had such a great sense of humor and showmanship—I wouldn't be surprised if he didn't plant somebody in the audience just to faint at a moment of high tension in the show. As a matter of fact, one time in London we had a lady from the Humane Society come backstage and threaten to close the show because we had sacrificed a white cock. I couldn't change her mind. She just wouldn't believe that the white cock in a number called *Shango* was a stuffed one and, at the same time, symbolic; but she created a commotion in the theater. Of course, this got in the papers and then ticket sales went way up. But this is the sort of thing Hurok would do. So I know that my legs were insured. I would be inclined to think with Lloyds of London because their rates were pretty high. He may have gone up as far as $250,000. I didn't know why it would be my legs, why it just wouldn't be my person, but it was a good publicity thing. A lot of people set more value on my legs than I did. I just never paid much attention to them, but they did apparently attract a lot of attention in the show.

Q. There were three women who were supposed to have the best legs in the world—you and two others. Who were the other two?

A. Let me see—I think I've heard that one, too. I know Mistinguette was one, and I suppose Marlene Dietrich was the other.

Q. You said in your book Island Possessed *that Damballa is a jealous god and would always be present in your life. And you've spoken about people that you've worked with who have been jealous of your stardom, such as the late Josephine Baker and Ethel Waters.*

A. Well, Ethel Waters in *Cabin in the Sky* was a great problem to me and I admired her so much, but at the same time she was the star of the show without question. I was fighting to hold my own in a field that I knew not at all, the field of musical comedy which included not only dancing, but acting and singing. At the same time I was keeping the company together. I didn't feel I was willing to be overshadowed simply because she was the star of the show.

Ethel Waters was a difficult person, and I think it was because of her experience in all-white Broadway theater. She's one of the greatest actresses I've known, and I still don't think she ever came into her own or did what she should have done. I would like to have seen her doing serious dramatic roles such as Lady Macbeth, but because she was black she didn't. I think she knew this and it made her feel frustrated, so at times she showed these frustrations through her nervous tension. I realize now that anyone with a star's responsibility operates under the kind of tension that sometimes appears to be jealousy or what we think of as a "difficult character."

I would say that Ethel Waters did exhibit a certain amount of jealousy—not just toward me, but toward the whole company. When you're starring and some other person or group of persons can get just as much applause as you do at a certain time, I think everyone has a certain jealous feeling. I know *I* would. This is the way I felt when Avon Long stole the show in *Carib Song*, but it didn't keep me from realizing that I had learned a great deal from Ethel Waters. The natural jealousy of a star to a rising star was there in *Cabin in the Sky*.

As far as Josephine Baker was concerned, I think that our presence in Paris created a psychological reaction in her. For one thing, it was shortly after the war and she had not been appearing so much. Also, I'm not at all sure that she was at that time as much in favor with the Parisian public as she had been before. Anyway, our coming opened a whole new theatrical vista for her. As she told me at the time, our appearances spurred her on to open her own club and appear more. She certainly was one of the most loved people in European theater and had held an undisputed position as a star in some of the same fields in which I operated. She excelled in dancing, acting, singing, and in a kind of total theater, although she performed for the most part in the various music halls. So I think that Josephine Baker's immediate reaction was probably to accept us as a challenge in her own field. As we got to know each other, we became friends. Everytime we performed in the same town, we made certain to make time to see each other. She called me her "sister." I think we had a very good relationship—whatever jealousy existed, I'm sure, must have been mine as well as hers.

Q. Is it true that while you were appearing in the Far East, impressarios, the press, and even the general public couldn't enter your dressing room until they removed their shoes?

A. Yes, that was one of those things. Even before we got to Australia, Japan, and into the East, I had become interested in Japanese music and customs. Therefore, in getting ready to tour Japan, I decided to have a Japanese dressing room. (Periodically I changed my dressing room—if we were in Italy, I would hang some Michelangelo prints to effect a certain Italian feeling, or in Mexico or Spain do a similar thing.) I like to arrange dressing rooms, rearrange them as I would my living room. So I got ready for the Orient by preparing a Japanese room with *shoji* screens and a *tatami* on the floor. I was fastidious about keeping the floor clean. One good reason for this habit was that I was barefoot most of the time. I always carried some sort of floor covering—this time it was a Japanese *tatami*.

My husband helped me make my dressing room into a small, very elegant, charming Japanese room. I kept the dressing table at a low level and had chairs with some cushions—it was very Japanese. I decided that neither I nor anyone else would be allowed to walk in there with shoes on. It wasn't sanitary, nor was it ethnically correct. So I would always take my shoes off and take from my dresser special sandals to slip into and straw sandals for visiting guests. Some entered in their stocking feet, while others would stay in the doorway and not come in at all. This arrangement was great because it kept my dressing room from being overrun with people, as it frequently was at the end of the show. I would even explain to the impressario, no matter who it was, "Please forgive me, but I would rather that you put these slippers on, or I'll step out if you wait a minute."

I remember one reporter who was very relucatant to take off his shoes. I found that he had a hole in his socks, so I called for a needle and thread and, while he interviewed me, I darned his socks.

Q. In regard to Ballet Folklorico of Mexico, is it true that you were the first one to introduce that idea to the Mexican people?
A. I think that this happened in many countries of the world, Mexico and Argentina being the best examples. When we first went to Mexico in 1947, as nearly as I remember, the Mexicans had no concept of a kind of dance–theater that utilized folk material and folk tradition to form a ballet that would tell the history of the Mexican

people. I would say that we strongly influenced the ballets coming out of Mexico, but this would also be true of a number of other countries.

Q. Is it true that you were intimately associated with Haitian presidents?
A. Three of them I knew quite well. I wrote about this in *Island Possessed*. I knew Dumarsais Estimé very well, Paul Magloire and his wife fairly well, and Duvalier, the father Duvalier, to some degree. Duvalier with his officers and his wife have visited our home in Haiti, at Leclerc. I had a number of audiences with him before his death. In the book *Island Possessed*, I wrote what I thought of these men, and what I thought had motivated their political actions and behavior.

All, in my opinion, were strongly motivated by culture heroes: Estimé identified with Toussaint L'Ouverture, Magloire with Christophe, and Duvalier with Dessalines.

Q. About how many performances would you say you missed during your many years of touring?
A. Only two, I can tell you about those two. This is a matter of maybe forty years' touring and appearing. With me, being onstage was always the important thing. "Be there, be there ahead of time, and be ready!" Now I'll tell you about two times when this didn't work out, and both were a great shock to me. For a number of years I've had nightmares about this sort of thing happening again. We were in Quito, Ecuador in the early fifties, and the president of Ecuador had been one of the Latin American ambassadors and presidents who had found a certain kind of pleasure, fraternity, and freedom in visiting the Dunham School on Forty-third Street. (That was our first school which I told you about.) The president, whose name was Paz (as nearly as I can remember), knew of my interest in anthropology and collecting artifacts, and after a personal audience had invited me to go to Esmeraldas, one of the coast towns of Ecuador.

Ecuador, as you know, was situated at a very high altitude. I think it's around twelve or thirteen thousand feet high. This meant taking a small army plane and going through the Andes, which is a fantastic experience. We then went down the coast across from Esmeraldas in dug-out canoes before crossing a very treacherous, rapid river into the town. The president had thought that here I would find remnants of black African culture. And sure enough, when I arrived the people who had known we were coming had assembled the drummers, who played something I had never seen before—hanging drums. Some of the drums resembled French or Spanish military drums more than African ones, but they had African drums, too. I became so involved in what they were doing that I missed a departure deadline at 3:00 in the afternoon. The skies were bright, and the mountains surrounding us certainly appeared to be innocent. We had stayed overtime maybe about a half hour, against the advice of the lieutenant who had been put in charge of the flight by the president. There were four of us including Lenwood Morris, Gordon Simpson (who took pictures), and my husband, John Pratt. I don't remember who else was there. But at 4:00 when we finally crossed this great treacherous river and were ready to pick up our plane to go back, the lieutenant announced that the take-off was not possible due to weather conditions. Well, to us everything looked cheerful and bright, and we couldn't understand why we couldn't fly out. To top this impossible situation, I guess some of the truth (as opposed to the mythology) about my authoritarian personality be- came evident, for I said, "This cannot be. We have to be back. We have a performance tonight." I tried to throw a little weight around, but it didn't do any good.

Along about 5:00 I insisted on getting some answers from the president's palace through the plane radio. I was still trying to get back. It was a short trip and a dangerous one, but at that time I didn't know it. At 7:00 the answer came that the president was not in—he had gone to see Madame Dunham in her performance at what- ever theater it was. Well, I thought I would collapse. It was just a ghastly experience for me and I tried my best to speak to the presi- dent and have him tell these stubborn (I thought) army lieutenants to take us back. But later I saw it couldn't possibly have been done without our having crashed in the Andes. Fortunately, they absolute- ly refused to be swayed by any ruse that I could bring into play.

We then had to cross the river again, at night, which was no fun, and stay in some strange little town at some tiny hotel. The only thing that comforted me was that Thor Heyerdahl's Kon-Tiki expedition had set forth from that point into the Pacific, so it was interesting to know that as far as accommodations were concerned, they had probably experienced many of the same things we had. But that was one of the two times I missed a performance.

The second time I missed a performance was when I had my appendix out in Jamaica. I had been ailing, you might say, all through South America. I knew that something was wrong, but I didn't know what. I had ignored my doctor's advice about not taking new sorts of medication, like cortisone. Cortisone at that time was a new treatment used for any arthritic pain, and I had previously undergone the gold-fever treatment for arthritic pain in Buenos Aires, Argentina. So I kept on taking cortisone in order to keep moving. Finally, in Jamaica, the effect of the drug hit me. We opened and in the beginning things seemed to go well. Jamaica was a place where I had always wanted to perform. I had wanted to return to the island where I had done my earliest research to let friends I had known many years before know I was alive and visiting their island once again.

We were having dinner with my friend, Fred Allsop, when all of a sudden I felt sharp pains like appendicitis pains. There I was. The show had to go on. Frantically we had to get in touch not only with the performers in the company, but a hospital. This was done while I lay in a daze, my appendix about to burst. They finally managed to get me into the hospital and into surgery. The company appeared for the first time without me onstage. I must say that I will always respect and admire that company, particularly Lenwood Morris and Vanoye Aikens standing in. The show was immediately assembled. I think I told you before that we carried a lot of baggage with us for a number of shows, at least three different shows, that were interchangeable. But a show went on that night in Jamaica and, when I awoke after surgery, I was a little annoyed to know that it had gone on very well without me and that the reviews were fantastic. Whereas in Esmeraldas, Ecuador the show simply *couldn't* go on without Lenwood, who was the star and with us on the trip—as a result the show had to be cancelled—in Jamaica, the show *did* go on.

I've given you these two instances of when I have missed shows which were, I would say, two of the roughest experiences in my life. I think that if you're performing you should be there.

Q. Do you ever drink before a performance?

A. No, but I'd say that during the first half of my career I would have a drink after the show once in a while. As pressures began to increase, I would drink at the second intermission, and as they increased more, at the first intermission. I have never been one to drink before a show, but I think if I had kept on for another few years it would have happened. But the fact I *did* drink (and I hope to goodness it was never done to an extent the audience could feel it) gave a little license to the company. I have remembered seeing a curtain go up, knowing that one or two company members really shouldn't have been onstage (this is toward the later years when, I suppose, if there is any excuse at all to drink, it would be from the exhaustion of constant touring). I would stand in the wings and seeing this, be deeply embarrassed. Whether the audiences noticed or not I don't know. But that tendency existed in the Dunham Company. I think I could even say the racial and economic background of company members was a cause. Frequently our paths crossed those of jazz entertainers and musicians. While we never had the dope problem that many bands had, the tendency in the company to gravitate after hours to this particular element was there. After all, we were not a ballet company, and many of us had friends in these bands. By the nature of their work, the musicians in clubs of Paris, New York, and other cities would be up long after we finished a show and would be drinking, so our company would join in. I wouldn't say that my company members picked up their habits— nevertheless, it was one of those occupational things. Under the pressure of touring it affected, now and then, some members' performances. This deeply embarrassed me—it probably kept me from overindulging.

One personal experience I can vividly remember, and I'll hasten to say it happened while we were in Stockholm. As a matter of fact there were two, but one of them did not affect a performance. In Stockholm I was in a benefit performance at the theater. Now although I had heard of tequila and other drinks, I'd never had any experience with the Swedish liqueur aquavit. Like vodka it was served cold, and I was hot, tired, and thirsty during the performance and drank more than I should have. Vanoye Aikens still tells how I

began singing "C'est Lui" so off-key there was no returning to its
proper melody. Nobody could save the situation. I remember being
aware that something was wrong. I was so glad to get to the dance
where I knew he could cover for me. That was one of my experiences
with drinking.

The other one occurred after a performance at the opening of
the first U.N. conference in San Francisco. I was invited to a Russian
party. I don't know if it was at the embassy or at a U.N. delegate
mission. We came to the party—which was actually given, to some
degree, in our honor—late because of the performance. There were
huge carved ice figures in bowls, boats of caviar (which at that time I
didn't eat), etc. But more than that, bottles and bottles of vodka just
stood frozen into ice boats. So again I was thirsty and drank. I left
not really knowing what had happened. In my version of the story I
was going to the ladies' room on the second floor, then going
through a large salon where, I insisted, on every wall was a picture of
Stalin. Somebody later said that was not true, that there was only
one picture, and I said, "No, I saw one on *every* wall." Those are two
experiences that I most vividly remember where I could have
embarrassed the company.

> *Q. Is it true that you were the first concert dancer to ever dance bottom-*
> *less, although it was by accident?*

A. Yes, I suppose it was true. I have a habit of forgetting things when
I go onstage and, although I say it may be a Freudian slip, I most
frequently forgot my underpants. When we first appeared at Lincoln
Center in Chicago after my return from the West Indies, I was doing
a nautch dance with turns, which had been inspired by Vera Mirova,
one of my teachers in Oriental dancing. While I was turning I felt
sort of a breeze—you know, when your skirts should go out at a 45°
angle—and it felt a little chilly. Suddenly it dawned on me I had forgotten to put on my underpants. So I slowed down my turns and
movements to allow the skirts to flow at a lesser angle. After that the
people in the company teased me. But this happened more than
once, partly because I would frequently wear elastic stockings in a
number, and over these, of course, for modesty's sake, a pair of
briefs. But on a number of occasions I have forgotten the briefs and

have been once again reminded by the company, who could always tell before the audience could.

Q. Being a true Cancerian, a home lover, how did you feel about living on the road, in and out of suitcases?

A. Well, there was a certain amount of compensation. The stage, when it was hung with familiar curtains and lights, became my home. I was seldom in the theater later than two hours before a performance. Once or twice I came in one hour before and I think, once in my life, at a half hour before, which nearly caused me to totally collapse. I would always use the theater as home. I still think of it now and would like today to have a few minutes of lying on our platforms—you remember we always had portable platforms which were attached to steps, then placed upstage or in the middle of the stage. These were always swept completely clean, even in countries that didn't believe in cleanliness. There I would lie before a performance thinking about the show and truly feeling the stage as home.

As I mentioned before, I often changed my dressing room to conform with the aesthetic ideas of different countries we visited. My true love was my dressing room and stage. I had trunks that were put near my dressing room that contained my personal clothing, including a famous Louis Vuitton secretarial trunk that was lost. (There's a story about that—later it turned up somewhere in Hollywood, where it had been accidentally sold at an auction. We'd left it behind in moving. I finally traced and called the people who had bought it, and they were not willing to give it up.) When I opened my makeup trunk, my makeup table would be set and ready for me— even my changes of dressing gowns were designed to fit the country where we were touring. For instance, in the Far East I always wore a kimono. When the room was set up it usually had more fresh flowers than I could handle, and I felt at home. It bothered me to have to go to a hotel. Frankly, I think that when I left my dressing room to spend the night, it was in the way one would leave home to go on a day's vacation. My real home, my Cancerian house, was my dressing room.

Q. How did you face loneliness, fatigue, discouragement, and success on the road.

A. I don't think I did too well with fatigue. I reacted. Once I think I made a little note somewhere in some of my many, many notes that fatigue is one of the bitterest enemies of man. I used to fight it as I could with medication, or with simply breaking my schedule for one day followed by staying in bed for the next. But, as I look back, I didn't do this often enough. I suffered from fatigue and I drove myself. I drove myself to always be there for a performance—not only a performance, but maybe just a rehearsal.

When it came to loneliness, it was hard for me to feel lonely with the company around. I knew what it was like not to communicate with them or not to be able to communicate with them in the way that I would have liked, say, as I would with a close friend or an analyst. But I couldn't really feel lonely because I knew there was always an 8:30 curtain preceded by a knock on my door when Lenwood Morris would look in, or Vanoye Aikens would pass by, or Lucille Ellis, or Gloria Thornburg, or someone else in the company. I didn't feel lonely, although I sometimes felt I was out on a kind of limb, that they didn't understand me or that I didn't really understand myself. These were occasions when I felt I had overextended myself and had gone farther than I should have, and that as a result our communication was left up to circumstance. But I never wanted to put the burden of my personal problems or failures onto the company. I would seldom go to them with things that were troubling me, even when some of them suspected something was wrong. I think a deep loneliness on a deep level is the inheritance of anyone who is creative.

Q. How did you feel about members leaving the company at inconvenient times?

A. That happened frequently. I've always said that two of man's greatest curses are envy and blackmail. I won't say that on some occasions they didn't leave because it was "their time"; yet at other times I felt they simply left because they would try to force from me some kind of compromise that I was not willing to give. If we were performing in this country I would have fewer problems, i.e., fewer discipline problems, or problems with people leaving because they were never indispensable and could at least be replaced. But just imagine being in Argentina or Australia or as far away as you can imagine. My policy always was (and I think I was supported in this by the union) that if you're going to leave, give me notice. I said to them, "Give me however much time is required—you pay your return fare, and I'll pay for a replacement." Well, this arrangement didn't work. I'd find somebody wanting to leave who wouldn't be prepared to pay their own fare, much less help me to find a replacement. If I tried to bring up the subject of the correct thing to do according to union contract, I'd get a call from the American Embassy where the person had gone claiming to be wronged by contract. Either this would happen or they would declare themselves indigent and ask the embassy to pay their fare, and so forth and so on. A lot of times these people had far more in cash or savings than I had. So their leaving became quite a problem. But it's one of the reasons the company ended up nonsolvent or stayed nonsolvent (as usually was the case).

I would also replace people when they began to cause trouble. Often I had done my best to reconcile whatever had gone wrong. But many times it just couldn't be, and sometimes they simply wanted to leave because they had other jobs in mind.

It was a very awkward time in Paris when Eartha Kitt left. I was extremely upset because I thought she could have at least completed our season. But now, reflecting on it, I realize it was her time to go. She had seen London and Paris and, in observing me, knew what being a star was like. She was also aware of her own talent as a dancer. Her acting talent was something that was noticed later—I believe by Orson Welles—but certainly her mime talent, her dance, and much of her vocal talent had been put before the public—at least in the beginning—by us. She had really become a featured part of the company, so it was very difficult for us to have her leave with practically no notice.

Since then I've talked with her and with many others who have gone out on their own, sometimes with success and sometimes not, beginning with Talley Beatty and Janet Collins who left us in California. But I see that this was, after all, part of what I believe in. We've always been a dance education institution—I couldn't be a dance educator unless I developed leaders, and once developed as leaders, there's no particular reason why their careers should continue within the Dunham Company. That type of company becomes too much like a cult, which I've never really approved of.

Q. Have the feelings of those who have left remained strained, or has the tension eased off in later years?

A. For a long while I would encounter people for whom I had rid all feelings of resentment, yet who would act very uncomfortable with me. I think it would have to do with the manner in which they left. I think sometimes that their feelings of guilt were stronger than my feelings of resentment, and that as a result their feelings took a long time to change. For instance, in Eartha Kitt's case, I don't know anyone who has been more vocal over her admiration of me, of the company, and of what she received from the company. Furthermore, I don't think she's ever been on a television talk show without mentioning me or the company. Those are the things that count.

I don't think it's that momentary breach, but whether or not people are adult enough to see, understand, and carry on afterwards. I would say now that the company no longer exists—practically everyone who may have had feelings of resentment or guilt or negative feelings in general has had time to grow up. Out of the blue sky someone will phone me just for old times' sake, as Eddie Clay did a couple of weeks ago from California. Or I'll receive a note and frequently read some comment such as "I didn't realize how important this experience was until much later in my life." Or someone else will say, "The experience really made me not so much a professional, but a human being and a person as well." And others will say, "Now I understand as I didn't before—now I understand much more." This is the way it should be, and I feel very good about their reactions.

Q. How do you feel about people using your technique without giving any credit to you or lifting parts of your choreography?

A. Well, I don't like this. For a long time I just refused to watch other dancers perform after I performed because I didn't wish to be tempted to use some movement from *their* choreography. But because I feel productive, I'm not all bitter about plagiarism. I think as a creative person you feel continuously productive, and as a result you look on the fact that people will perhaps use your material as being rather logical. On many occasions I've had the uncomfortable feeling that, because we traveled abroad so much, we were sort of an easy target for plagiarism. Hollywood copied some of my husband's costumes; someone else in Hollywood imitated some of my mannerisms and numbers; Broadway choreographers lifted out certain things (I can still see some of them on television). I'm just happy that I'm not one who needs to plagiarize. I'm also happy I was not here when it happened. When I returned from our tours, I would meet people on the street who would look at me as if saying, "Well, is she *still* here?" or "Is she back to stay?" We really nourished Broadway and Hollywood for a long time, and I'm not the least embarrassed to say it.

I particularly don't like people who avoid giving credit to the Dunham technique because this is one thing that was mine to develop and give. I've always said, "I'm proud that I'm from the University of Chicago," and I should think anyone would be proud if they stayed with the Dunham Company long enough to make it their career. I think that getting around things by saying "I'm teaching technique" when I ask, "What technique? It's got to be some kind of technique," is wrong. But they avoid using the words "Dunham technique."

If they're going to teach ethnic dancing, they've got to cover a tremendous field—most teachers don't. If they're simply teaching primitive rhythms in dance or folk rhythms in dance, it's usually second-hand. I found that, toward the latter days of our touring, many schools sprang up. Then, because there was work on television, many small companies were formed. At that time a need to use this material existed. Although these teachers and performers recognized the value of the Dunham technique, they did not see the need to give credit where it should have been given. I suppose, for personal reasons, I was really quite shocked. Even now, in my efforts to explain what the Dunham technique *is*, I realize I should have written more about it. Maybe this would have protected both the technique and the choreography from being plagiarized.

> *Q. These two questions can be asked together: Are you a strong disciplinarian, and did you frequently interrupt performances to discipline the company?*

A. I'm not as strong a disciplinarian now as I used to be. I would say that today I take a completely different attitude toward discipline. While touring, I felt pressed for time and perfection and knew we simply could not waste energy on bad, apathetic, or sloppy performances. We simply had to reach a certain perfection. I know that a part of this discipline was administered in an attempt to destroy the myth that black people don't have discipline. So I felt that we really were not super-disciplined, but highly disciplined within a certain kind of freedom. I think this gave dynamism to the company.

In choreography or in performance, I never wanted to make an individual conform to the extent that the individual no longer existed. Often I've argued with people who think that in choreography dancers are simply like chess pawns to be moved around. I think that keeping the individual personality and casting the individual to be sure that the choreography suits the person, so that they are happy in what they are doing, is of the utmost importance. I also think that I tried to observe certain strict disciplinarian regulations. If I found myself becoming like a policeman, I would call the company together and say, "Look, I'm not here to criticize you because it makes me happy or because I'm being sadistic. *You've* got to see why these changes have to be—otherwise we can't have a company." This worked pretty well. Yes, it was a highly disciplined company.

Today I still discipline, but with a different approach which prepares the student for the life of real professional and sometimes even social competition. Discipline takes time. That's why we teach to our young people in East St. Louis a program called "Socialization Through the Arts." We hope that this course will cause people to become more aware of themselves. I have to be extremely patient, as does anyone who teaches in this or a similar setting. I think that's one of the things I have learned in East St. Louis. Sometimes people who have known me before or master teachers from the company who now teach with me feel that I am permissive. After trying to defend myself in terms of the setting we're presently in, I finally have to say, "Well, I'm not too sure that there's anything wrong with being permissive."

I think to a certain degree one has to be permissive. We're no longer under pressure to travel, tour, perform, or enter into competition with other touring companies in the capitals of the world. We don't have to do that. So I think there has to be a slower method. That's what I'm working on now. I now have people discipline themselves and do things because they feel that they must do them—not, as frequently happened before, because I say, "This is what you must do and if you don't understand it, do it anyway, because *I* say so and *I* have the responsibility for it."

I don't use that method of discipline anymore. But at every intermission (we had two fifteen-minute intermissions which in emergencies would sometimes run into half-hours) I would, whether onstage, in the wings, or in the dressing rooms, if anything went wrong from the orchestra pit right down to the whole stage crew, call the company onstage to discuss it. Over the years this became their training in direction, in staging, in choreographing, and in many cases, in performing arts management and administration. During intermissions I would criticize and point out the things that were not satisfactory to me in the performance, and I would do so in no uncertain terms, and sometimes under great pressure and tension.

Q. Could that have been where the myth or truth came that Dunham dancers hated you?

A. It could very well have been. I think that I remember reading that statement in *Jet* magazine at one time, and I was absolutely stunned. I couldn't believe it because no matter what they said or *if* they said, "She's a so-and-so" or "Who does she think she is?" or "I'm not gonna do this or that," I didn't pay much attention. I knew that underneath it all, even though they might go out to some bar at night to talk about me in terms that I wouldn't have been happy about at all, or speak with their friends, or complain, or even say unpleasant or bitter things, I couldn't pay too much attention. I felt they were staying—they were working and they were giving so much. This just seemed a reaction to some feeling of sibling rivalry which was then rampant in the company. I'll always remember something Harry Belafonte once said, "You know, you certainly are a peculiar woman. They used to come back from a tour and they'd tell me, 'I'm not going back to that—no matter what happens, I'm through

with the whole thing.' And they'd be so sure of it. A few weeks later
I'd see someone running down the street with a telegram waving in
their hand. I'd say, 'What is it?' and they'd say, 'She sent for me!'"

So I think that's the way things really worked. I think this thing
of "why they hate Dunham" is far more subtle. I think it has to do
with how frustrated company members felt in not really understanding me.

Q. How did you feel about the two closings of your schools in New York?
A. The first closing was a great shock and was one of the milestones
in my decision to give up the company. I will probably never again
invest emotionally and even financially as I had in the first big Dunham school in New York. I felt that its closing was terribly unjust.
I had lost the director, Syvilla Fort, because she went to work in and
develop her own school. More than anything, I could not find
enough American money to keep it, chiefly because of the cost of
transferring funds in foreign countries. At the time, the company was
on tour. Getting the krones, marks, lire, or pesos converted into
dollars had to be done on the black market at a great loss, and to
have this returned to the school on a monthly basis was impossible.
The rent for the school was not high, nor were its operating costs,
but it needed constant financing. There was hardly a year that went
by that didn't have ten, twenty, or twenty-five thousand dollars
invested by me to keep it running. It was never a school that paid for
itself, and I felt terribly disappointed when the general public would
not rise to its aid and when foundations would not give it support.
It was valuable, I thought then, and I still think so. I didn't feel that I
alone should carry its deficit. It got to the point where I was running
too far behind. Even though the owner, Lee Shubert, was a friend,
our rent would frequently be several months past due. I felt very
badly about that.

The second New York school opened after *Bamboche* closed. I
opened it around mid-1962 or early 1963, but I did not have much
faith in it. By then I realized a strange thing. Say a Broadway show
would want to rehearse and need rehearsal space. The shows all
followed certain patterns and went to certain established commercial
schools to rent rehearsal space even though ours was more pleasant,
cleaner, and more charming. Even black shows that were rehearsing

ignored our school. That rent would have helped us a great deal economically.

When it came to students, already the beginnings of students' getting something for nothing such as lessons, which developed during the late sixties and early seventies, was taking place. As a result, we found many young people who thought they were able to study anywhere and get their lessons subsidized by the government—and more than that, they frequently wanted to be paid to take lessons by some student program. (This is our practice today in East St. Louis.)

As a result of the students' attitude, I didn't find the second New York school's closing nearly as draining. It didn't have "part of me" invested in it to the extent of the first school. When Lucille Ellis, its director, had to resign because her parents were ill in Chicago, I knew I couldn't continually commute between East St. Louis and New York to replace her. I couldn't find another person to run it and, although I would have been willing to continue investing in it, it just wasn't practical. Finally, I returned to New York and saw to it that everything was packed. The bars and mirrors from that second school are currently being used by our classes here in East St. Louis.

Q. Is it true that you were in jail within the first night of your arrival in East St. Louis?

A. Yes, it's true. Jeanelle Stovall, my assistant, and I came into the city to begin interviewing students. I had been coming into East St. Louis by day and driving back to Alton, Illinois, where I was based with some of my archives, before dark. I came every day. But this time we had to stay after dark because I was interviewing some members of the Warlord gang and other youths whom I hoped would become members of our training program within the university.

We interviewed in various neighborhood centers where these young people come together, and immediately we had a following of young militants. They were off deep into something that even they perhaps weren't sure about—the idea of a newcomer in town who was interested in them and interested in them having minimum subsistence. This idea appealed to them. I think at that time we had a certain amount of OEO [Office of Economic Opportunity] work-money that they could have had if they would just come to the university to dance and take martial arts. Of course being trained in karate and percussion was top priority to them.

So we had to stay after dark to locate some of these young people that we wanted to sign up because we had a deadline in the next day or two. We stopped in a bar with some of them and were crossing the street on our way home. It was quite dark, probably 8:00 or 9:00, and I was saying to Jeanelle, "Now don't forget, tomorrow we start at the Warlord Center." I turned around and found I was talking to no one. A police car had pulled up and all these young men were being hauled into it.

Stovall and I went over to the police car right away and demanded to know what was going on. The police were very rude and said, "None of your business. Who are you?" I said, "Well, I think that we ought to find out what's going on. Why are you just picking up people like that?"

The city was burning—the sky was red with fires left and right. There were police cars, sirens, stoplights, headlights—all these intimidations and they were picking up the young men. I was horrified.

Stovall and I drove to the police station; there I saw a couple of Warlords that I had talked with earlier. I said, "What is going on?" They answered, "Well, this is what's been going on: There's a fire in town; they pick up all the young people they can; they don't ask questions or anything."

I said to one of them, "Listen, you go back there on the corner where we were earlier, find some of your friends, and get 500 to 1000 people in this town to sit on the steps of this jail and protest."

Well, that didn't work out. A number of protesters came, but with a certain amount of intimidation. This sort of action, to my knowledge, had never before been taken in East St. Louis. Jeanelle and I stormed into the police station's inner office where there were a few black cops, but mostly big, tough-looking Irish cops, and I said, "What is going on?" They said, "Lady, you shut up if you know what's good for you."

Of course, that's all they needed to say to me. So we went in to see the night chief of police, who happened to be black—I think I can now say colored—and started protesting again. "I'm going to tell Washington," I said, and I threw out other places and names. I hardly knew what I was saying, I was so outraged. When I came out of the police chief's office, Jeanelle was there, stripping off all of her rings and jewelry. I said, "What are you doing?" She said, "I've been arrested."

"For what?"

"Because I told these men they couldn't do this. That the Warlords had to have legal representation." The place was then packed with young men waiting to be put into cells.

I told the police, "I want to phone my lawyer."

"Well, you'll call no one."

"You mean to say you don't have legal representation for people?"

"After twenty-four hours we'll see what we're going to do."

"Oh no, you won't." There was a little gate behind the desk barring the entrance to a room where a lot of policemen stood. I pushed my way through the gate and said, "All right, if you want to arrest somebody, arrest me."

A hefty, Irish, red-faced cop said, "You get out of here."

"I'm not going to get out of here, and if you try to put me out of here you're going to be in trouble."

So he shoved me and I shoved back at this great, huge hunk of Irish flesh and muscle. It was like shoving against a brick wall or a bulwark. This man grabbed my arm and twisted it. I said, "All right, am I arrested?"

"Are you satisfied? You want to be arrested? Yes, you are."

I said, "That's exactly what I wanted." So I went out to the desk and stripped myself of my jewelry. I saw a group of black policemen and said, "You certainly ought to be ashamed of the way you earn your living."

That was the most vitriolic thing I could think of at the moment. They just laughed at me.

I said, "I want a doctor."

One of them said in a very seductive manner, "Lady, I'll be your doctor."

Well, that really infuriated me. So we spent the night in jail. It was nerve-wracking because we could see the flames through the narrow windows. There was no electric light and no water at all for any purpose whatsoever in the cell. We could see the police guards walking up and down with their cups of coffee and snacks. We asked for some water and the policeman on patrol told us, "shut up." I told Jeanelle, "Let's just be philosophical." We then stretched out on the dining table in the middle of the room because the bunks looked too dirty. It was a dirty tin table, but we stretched out and I said, "I'm just going to wait it out, that's all. I just hope the militants don't decide to burn down the jail. But our friends know we're in here, so I don't think they will. Besides, all our friends are here. I hope the jail doesn't accidentally catch on fire."

Meanwhile, my daughter, who had just returned from Europe and didn't speak English very well, had been with us when we were snatched in and didn't know what was happening. She was befriended by a Lutheran priest who went to the jail every night to see what was going on and how he could help. So he took her home to my husband in Alton. Later, some of the Warlords went to Alton and got John, who got busy on lawyers. Finally, about four o'clock in the morning somebody said we could go down and swear to the judge, whom they had made get out of bed to come there, that we were guilty.

I said, "Guilty of what?"

"Well, disorderly conduct."

By then they had given us back our jewelry. I said, "No, here, take these things back again. I'll just wait here until I can get some justice."

"Well, you don't have to pay anything—you can sign on your own recognizance."

I didn't know what that meant, but said, "I'm signing nothing!"

We started back towards the cells, and as I reflect on the situation, it was very funny. The judge and the police started pleading, "Now, you've got your chance to go, why don't you all act like nice girls and leave?"

"Why should I? You want me to sign something that's not true. I should say not. When I start talking, I'm going to talk an awful lot and it's going to get to Washington, too. So, just let me stay in here."

Well, finally they refused to put us back in jail, so we went home. Three months later I was honored with the key to the city, given to me by the mayor.

Q. During the period of black awareness, how did you feel about having a white husband? How were you accepted?

A. Well, my first real indication of its intensity was in 1965 when we were in Harlem performing because somebody else had canceled out due to the race riots. Our conductor, along with some members of his orchestra, was white; the company had one white dancer; our wardrobe mistress and even my secretary were white. These were all people who traveled with us on world tours. At the time I really was anxious and worried.

I went to the theater manager and to the orchestra leader of one of the other orchestras in our show with a certain amount of concern. Everybody backstage took the stand that, since we had enough courage to come there to perform through some of the riot areas, they were going to see to it that we were protected. At that time, I felt concern for my husband. Fortunately he didn't have to be at the theater too often. The worst difficulty was transporting our own company members to the theater. They could take the subway and walk through these areas, but to get a taxi to go to Harlem was almost impossible. Whereas before discrimination had been over token things, such as a civil rights movement or integration of a school cafeteria, the race riots were really serious on a total level I hadn't previously bargained for.

After 1965 I went on various tours to Europe and Africa and, as I said before, it wasn't until I came to East St. Louis that racism and having a white husband really hit me full-force. For the first three years I was very, very anxious about my husband and had certain arguments with him because I would say categorically, "Do not sit in front of the window at night without pulling down the shade," or "Do not be on the streets after dark." He thought this was absolutely absurd until one time he was mugged and robbed in broad daylight as he came out of one of the supermarkets. Then he began to listen to my warnings.

Frequently I would scan the newspapers to see if anything had happened to our students or instructors. We began to notice that the situation was not so much *color* as it was *economics*. East St. Louis had finally changed from a white industrial center with so many Czechs, Irish, and Polish professionals in white-collar positions to a city with about ninety percent or more black population. After 5:00 P.M., when the banks and offices would close and white commuters would travel to the outskirts, East St. Louis became simply another black city.

In the beginning I was very anxious. I had been deeply involved with the militants—in a useful way, I hope. I think some of them were even saved from genocide by our active interest. Nevertheless, I had the embarrassment of having emergency meetings with them or any other counsel I could give them knowing that my husband could not be present. He felt the same way, so whenever there was an indication that I was going to such a meeting he would withdraw and go to his room. This upset me a little bit.

For years I have worked on a kind of third-world approach to education at PATC. As we began to have teachers who were Japanese or East Indian, or even black Africans and, from time to time, a few whites, the attitude toward race has changed. I would say that the training center and the city itself have been influenced by our relationship. Now both have a healthy attitude toward whatever color, national origin, or race you are, as long as your intentions are clear. And nobody is more sensitive to knowing a stranger's intention toward a city than people who are not formally educated. Many of the town's senior citizens have not gone vary far in school, but they have the kind of wisdom that frequently comes from people who can't read and write.

Q. Is your past life of performing and being a star still important to you?
A. I don't look back very much. I'm thinking now, "What next?" I'm very nostalgic, but I don't like it. I once wrote a story that began, "Nostalgia is the deadly charmer of my life." I don't like going back over old letters about what was, and living in the past. I have gradually trained myself out of it. I have enjoyed reading your book and seeing my life go before me through someone else's eyes, although in the past it would have upset me a little bit. I know it's logical to let

go, but the past charms you and makes you think you want to dream. But I don't think it's very positive—it's no good.

Q. What are your leisure interests now?

A. I'm interested in reading. I'm reading biographies. I remember Erich Fromm saying, "If you're ever feeling insecure or depressed, read about other people's lives." I've been wandering among all these books [at Habitation Leclerc, where part of this interview took place, every suite has one wall filled with books] and I've just selected an autobiography of Nehru, and am just finishing one of Gandhi. I like historical novels and science fiction. I *love* science fiction. Even while touring I read after returning at night to the hotel. Sometimes I became so engrossed in a novel that I would try to read snatches of it during a performance. I also painted in this way and would often arrive onstage with splashes of paint on my hands. It was an effort, I think, to escape loneliness. But more than this, I wanted to escape into something where the main actor was not the company. I had to feel that I existed in another life without them. I had to know that they didn't have every bit of me tied up, without a means of escape.

Q. Is is true that you read tarot cards?

A. Yes, I have read tarot cards for some time. I was getting pretty good at it, too. I think that cards, like the coins you throw (*I Ching*, and that sort of thing) are conductors for your own ESP. I have learned that you can get all of the details from tarot cards, but unless you allow yourself to get in another kind of consciousness and become a "sensitive," you're not really reading them. I was getting to the stage where I could feel quite secure with whatever I said, however I interpreted the cards, when I got sidetracked by a Chinese divination which I stayed with for several years.

Q. Do you believe in astrology?

A. In my later life I have turned to my astrological chart to see how much my character was influenced or formed by my birthdate. I'm a Cancerian with a Leo moon and a Scorpio ascendant. These astrological aspects have formed my character. For instance I have the Cancerian love of home—I would barely be in a hotel suite or dressing room before I would put familiar home touches to work. I love good food. My husband John and his brother Davis are Cancerians, too.

Q. Do you miss the pressures of creating new works for the company?*
A. Now that I'm not choreographing, I am expressing my creativity at Habitation Leclerc as both interior and exterior designer. It is, however, the first time I have not been writing, lecturing, or doing choreography. I feel I am at a creative standstill even though I am creating now on a new and less important level. I hope I've not done my last choreography, but I don't feel the need or drive to do it now. I remember an incident in Japan that reinforces this theory.

I had published two books and had recently completed my third, *A Touch of Innocence* (which was my biggest writing effort), and thought I would continue to turn out one book a year. I went to a Chinese astrologer who said, "No, you will probably turn out not more than five in your lifetime." I said, "Oh no, you must be wrong—I know what I'm going to write." I have about four subjects I'm interested in, but I will probably write only one more book. That's why I'm so happy to have you write this biography. Otherwise some things I know would never be said and known.

I thought I would be thrilled to see my own books lined up on a bookshelf but, as with many other things, it's nice, but not totally necessary. Now I have written a total of five books. I look at *Kasamance* [Odarkai Books, New York, 1974], which I wrote in the hospital in about fifteen days—I'm thrilled to have it published, but now I take it for granted. Sometimes creative things I do don't seem to be a part of me. I look at Habitation Leclerc in this manner. It has practically been carved out of the hillside, and every detail has been done with love and great care. Some of the workers who had lived at Habitation Leclerc before I leased the land have been there twenty years, like Gachelin, our chief engineer. I know it has grown, and although I recognize this I still don't realize the complexity of the steps that were taken to make it be. It's a detachment like giving birth to a child—after you raise it you go on to other things.

Often I wonder how much of my work "gets done." Even my choreography was a mysterious process. When I completed it I would see it onstage, know I had done it, and would be thrilled and pleased, because I never put anything that wasn't my best onstage, but still I

*Dunham's latest choreographic work was to Scott Joplin's "The Entertainer" in 1975.

ask the questions, "Where did this come from?" or "How did I get to do this?" There is always a kind of wonderment in my life, so that if I found myself on the moon tomorrow, it wouldn't surprise me. I would probably be just as curious and be doing something just as creative and, hopefully, beneficial for mankind.

Q. Where do your creative energies go now?

A. I use creative energies to do more for and with myself. Mostly alone. I'm not too sure I know myself. I know myself deeply, intuitively, but I want to know and understand myself better. I try to read things to help in this endeavor. I would also like to continue to associate with movements and institutions that are trying to improve life. Like in South America, where I conducted a forum on choreology, and taught at the Institute of Ethnomusicology and Folklore. This interests me very much, and in the last few years I've called on my academic background more and more. I try not to start things that will cause me disillusionment. I like wisdom and I want to develop more. I like the creative things some governments are doing. I believe South America will cause a whole new wave of importance to cultural life and politics developing simultaneously as a way of living and developing national consciousness. Today I try to be more discriminating in selecting people as friends and acquaintances or in selecting missions or work for myself. In other words, I'm willing to limit myself and put energy into only one or two things at a time.

Q. How do you feel about aging?

A. I think I have reached a point in judging my own attitudes toward age where I can be positive and enjoy my remaining years for what I have done before. Like Bernard Berenson loved to say, "The only advantage youth has over age is aesthetic." I haven't gotten down to the aesthetics of it except to say I'm very concerned about being overweight. I am happy to find myself among the authorities in what I have done and have researched. I'm pleased with my age and hope it never causes me the inconvenience of being immobile or with severe health problems.

I haven't yet tackled the change of one's appearance with age. Having had to keep my image intact so long in the theater, I don't like to see it changing now. But from the point of view of life

satisfaction, I feel quite good about what the years have done. I am
not a youth enthusiast, yet I like to help them when I can. I love
children and young people, but I'm not one to turn over the running
of Habitation Leclerc to teenagers. I used to say to the militants,
"Don't leave your parents and grandparents out of the struggle—
keep them in the picture and get their support and you will learn
a great deal about how your ancestors are considered in Africa. I
think I got to them because not only East St. Louis, but also many
other black communities are run by the grandmothers. They have a
lot to do with deciding what happens to the young people. As for
myself, I simply think of myself without consideration for time—for
the time being, that's enough.

Katherine Dunham and Vanoye Aikens in *Batucada*, Paris (*from the collection of Katherine Dunham*)

Katherine Dunham and Vanoye Aikens in *Acaraje*, performed at Ciro's, Hollywood, 1955 (*from the collection of Katherine Dunham*)

Dora, performed at Ciro's,
Hollywood, 1955
(*from the collection
of Katherine Dunham*)

Katherine Dunham and Ava Gardner relaxing during the filming of *The Bible*, Italy, 1964 (*photo courtesy of Twentieth Century–Fox*)

Stormy Weather, 1943 (*photo courtesy of Twentieth Century–Fox*)

Cumbia, performed at Ciro's, Hollywood, 1955 (*from the collection of Katherine Dunham*)

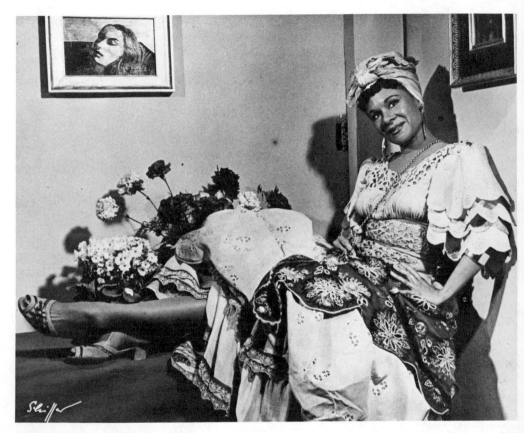

Katherine Dunham in her Sarah Bernhardt Théâtre dressing room, Paris, 1960, with Dunham's painting of Sylvana. Dunham is in costume for her role in *Acaraje* (*from the collection of Katherine Dunham*)

Stage Choreography by Dunham
(1937-1972)

This partial list of Dunham choreography was prepared by Katherine Dunham (to her best recollection), Jeanelle Stovall, and Vévé Clark. All dances not indicating place or date were choreographed in rehearsal and were not performed. This list also does not include the dates of PATCO productions originating in East St. Louis.

Acaraje, from *Hommage à Dorival Caymmi*, Arcachon, France, August 1952
Adeus Terras, Rome, 1949
Afrique, Rome, 1949
Afrique du Nord, Cave Supper Club, Vancouver, British Columbia, 1953
L'Ag'Ya, Federal Theatre, Chicago, January 27, 1938
        Ouverture; Market; Pas de deux; Zombie; Festival Scene
A las Montañas, Abraham Lincoln Center, Chicago, 1938. Solo concert only
        (first public singing). Played in October 1937 as part of *Péruvienne*
        with *A la Cenote*.
Amazon
Anabacoa, Chalfonte, Haddon Hall: Club Antilles, 1963
Angelique (or *Angelico* from *Haitian Suite*), Ciro's, Hollywood, 1948
Argentine Country Dances
Babalu, Curran Theatre, San Francisco, December 1941
Baby San
Bahiana, University of Cincinnati, Cincinnati, Ohio, 1939
Bajao
Bal Negre, New York and tour, 1946
Bamboche, 1962

Banana Boat, Empire Theatre, Manila, 1957
Banda
Barrelhouse, 1938
Batucada, Teatro Esperanza Iris, Mexico City, 1947
Big Ballet, from the film *Mambo*
Biguine–Biguine, 1937
Black Panther
Blues Trio, Ciro's, Hollywood, 1948
Bolero, Teatro Esperanza Iris, Mexico City, 1947
Boogie Woogie Prayer
Bre'r Rabbit an' de Tah Baby, Goodman Theatre, Chicago, 1938
Cakewalk, from *Bre'r Rabbit*, Goodman Theatre, Chicago, November 1938
Callate, Royal Alexandra Theatre, Toronto, Canada, January 1944
Caribbean Rhapsody
Carnaval, Broadway Theatre, New York, November 22, 1955
Carib Song, Adelphi Theatre, New York, October 1945
Caymmi (*Hommage à Dorival Caymmi*), Arcachon, France, August 1952
C'est Lui, Martinique Club, New York, 1947
Choros, first performed at Royal Alexandra Theatre, January 1944, Nos. 1–5
Ciudad Maravillosa, 1939
La Comparsa, from *Motivos*, Temple Theatre, Portland, Oregon (?), January 1946
Concert Rhumba, 1939
Congo Femme, from *Haitian Suite*, Curran Theatre, San Francisco, December
          1941
Cuban Danzon, Brooklyn Academy of Music, New York
Cumbancha, 1939
Cumbia, Cave Supper Club, Vancouver, British Columbia, 1953
Diablitos
Diamond Thief, New York, 1962
Dora, Cave Supper Club, Vancouver, British Columbia, 1953
Dos Hermanos
Doudou
Drum Ritual
Drum Session
Field Hands, from *Plantation Dances*, Windsor Theatre, New York,
          May 1940
Flaming Youth 1927, New Britain, Connecticut, February 1944
Floor Exercises, Dunham Experimental Group, Montclair Y.W.C.A., Montclair,
          New Jersey, November 7, 1947

Florida Swamp Shimmy, 1937

Floyd's Guitar Blues, Ciro's, Hollywood, 1955

Frevo, Paris, 1951

Haitian Roadside, Temple Theatre, Portland, Oregon, January 1946

Haitian Suite, Abraham Lincoln Center, Chicago, January 1937
            Congo Paillette; Yonvalou; Zepaules

Harry (Wild About. . .), Ciro's, Hollywood, 1955

Havana 1910/1919, (from *Promenade* in *Tropical Revue*, Opera House, San
            Francisco, March 1944

Honey in the Honeycomb, Cave Supper Club, Vancouver, British Columbia,
            1953

Honky Tonky Train, in *Le Jazz "Hot"*, Curran Theatre, San Francisco, Decem-
            ber, 1941

Hounci Canzo

Incantation, Cave Supper Club, Vancouver, British Columbia, 1953

Los Indios, Santiago de Chile, December 1950

Island Songs, Goodman Theatre, Chicago, 1938

Jazz Finale, Ciro's, Hollywood, 1955

Jazz in Five Movements, Théâtre National, Paris, March 1949

La Valse, Palacio de Bellas Artes, Mexico, 1947

Lazarus

Le Jazz "Hot" (includes *Boogie Woogie Prayer*, *Honky Tonky Train*, and *Barrel-
            house*), Goodman Theatre, Chicago, 1938

Lotus Eaters, 1937

Macumba, Ciro's, Hollywood, 1948

Madame Christoff (*Sarabande to Madame Christophe, Queen of Haiti*), Good-
            man Theatre, Chicago, October 1937

Maracas

Mexican Rumba, Goodman Theatre, Chicago, November 1938

Missouri Waltz, ca. 1948

Mozart

Nañigo, from *Motivos,* Temple Theatre, Portland, Oregon (?), January 1946

New Jazz

New Love, New Wine, Ciro's, Hollywood, 1955

Nibo from *Island Songs*, Goodman Theatre, Chicago, 1938

Nostalgia, Temple Theatre, Portland, Oregon (?), January 1946

Octoroon Ball, Mexico, 1947

Para Que Tu Veas, Royal Alexandra Theatre, Toronto, Canada, January 1944

Péruvienne, Goodman Theatre, Chicago, 1938

Plantation Dances, Windsor Theatre, New York, May 1940

Planting Rice, Manila, 1957

Preludios, Santiago de Chile

Processional

Quirino, from *Street Scene*, Prince of Wales Theatre, London, fall 1948

Ragtime, from *Nostalgia*, 1946. Performed as a separate piece at Ciro's, Hollywood, 1948

Ramona, Vocal group, Ciro's, Hollywood, 1952

Rara Tonga, originally the opening section of *Primitive Rhythms*, first performed at the Goodman Theatre, Chicago, October 1937. Performed as a solo at the Forrest Theatre, New York, November 1943

Rhumba Jive, Curran Theatre, San Francisco, 1941

Rhumba Rhapsody

Rhumba Suite, Curran Theatre, San Francisco, 1941

Rhumba Trio, Instituto Nacional de Bellas Artes, 1947

Rhumba Variations

Rites de Passage, Curran Theatre, San Francisco, December 1941
　　　　1. Puberty; 2. Fertility; 3. Death; 4. Women's Mysteries

Samba, *Brazilian Suite*, 1954

Saudade da Brazil, Goodman Theatre, Chicago, March 1938

Schulhoff Tango, Abraham Lincoln Center, Chicago, January 1937

Shango, from *Carib Song*, October 1945

Sister Kate, Manila Grand Opera Theatre, 1957

Son, from *Primitive Rhythms*, October 1938

Southland, Santiago de Chile, 1952 (?)

Spanish Earth Suite, Goodman Theatre, Chicago, 1938

Spirituals, Théâtre des Champs-Elysées, Paris, 1951

Street Scene, Prince of Wales Theatre, London, 1948

Strutters Ball, from *Plantation Dances*, Forrest Theatre, New York, November 1943

Tango, from *Jazz in Five Movements*

Ti' Cocomacaque, Sankei Hall, Tokyo, 1957

Tropics, Abraham Lincoln Center, Chicago, 1937

Tropical Revue, Forrest Theatre, New York, November 1943

Valse Creole

Veracruzana, Ciro's, Hollywood, 1948

Washerwoman, Paris, August 1952

Wine Door
Woman with a Cigar
Xaxado, from *Carnaval*, Broadway Theatre, New York, November 22, 1955
Yemaya, Ciro's, Hollywood, 1955

Musicals

Cabin in the Sky (collaboration with Balanchine), New York and tour, 1940–41
Pins and Needles, New York, 1940
Tropical Pinafore, Chicago, 1939
Windy City, Great Northern Theatre, Chicago, May 13, 1947
Les Deux Anges, Paris, 1965
Ciao, Rudi (artistic collaborator), Rome, 1965

Operas

Aïda, for the Metropolitan Opera, New York, 1964
Faust, for SIU, Carbondale, Illinois, 1965
Treemonisha, Atlanta, 1972

Film Choreography by Dunham

This list was researched and documented by Giovannella Zannoni.

Carnival of Rhythm　　1939, U.S.A.
　　　　Produced by Warner Brothers
　　　　Directed by Jean Negulesco
　　　　Color
　　　　Short twenty-minute film entirely dedicated to Katherine Dunham and
　　　　　　Company
　　　　Choreography by Katherine Dunham
　　　　Contains the following numbers from the Dunham repertoire:
　　　　　　Ciudad Maravillosa
　　　　　　Los Indios
　　　　　　Batucada
　　　　　　Adeus Terras

Pardon My Sarong　　1942, U.S.A.
　　　　Produced by Universal Pictures
　　　　Directed by E. C. Kenton
　　　　Color
　　　　Choreography by Katherine Dunham
　　　　No personal appearance by either Katherine Dunham or her company

Star Spangled Rhythm   1942, U.S.A.
    Produced by Paramount Pictures
    Directed by George Marshall
    Black and White
    Personal appearance by Katherine Dunham

Stormy Weather   1943, U.S.A.
    Produced by Twentieth Century Fox
    Directed by Andrew Stone
    Black and White
    Personal appearance by Katherine Dunham and Company
    Choreography for the Dunham Company by Katherine Dunham.

Casbah   1948, U.S.A.
    Produced by Universal Pictures
    Directed by John Berry
    Black and White
    Personal appearance by Katherine Dunham and Company
    Ramadan Festival and Casbah Nightclub choreography by Katherine
        Dunham

Botta e Risposta   1950, Italy
    Produced by Ponti–de Laurentiis
    Directed by Mario Soldati
    Black and White
    Personal appearance by Katherine Dunham and Company
    Contains the following numbers from the Dunham repertoire:
        Batucada
        Jazz in Five Movements (segment)
    The print is the property of De Laurentiis Cinematografica, Rome.

Mambo   1954, Italy
    Produced by Ponti–de Laurentiis for Paramount Pictures
    Directed by Robert Rossen
    Black and White
    Choreography by Katherine Dunham
    Personal appearance by Katherine Dunham and Company

Mambo (continued)

> Contains exclusive and rare footage of the Dunham Company in classroom demonstrations of the Dunham technique.
>
> The following five numbers were choreographed expressly for the film:
>> *Coboclo do Mato* (sung and danced by Katherine Dunham)
>> *Baiao* (never performed onstage)
>> *Sube Espuma* (danced by Katherine Dunham—later performed onstage in a different version)
>> *New Love, New Wine*
>> *Mambo* (performed onstage in a different version under the title of *Mambo Finale*)
>
> The print is the property of Dino de Laurentiis Cinematografica, Rome. A copy is also available in the United States through Paramount Pictures.

Liebes Sender   1954, Germany

> Black and White
>
> Personal appearance by Katherine Dunham and Company
>
> Contains the following numbers from the Dunham repertoire:
>> *Choros* (No. 1 and No. 4)
>> *Shango*
>> *Tropics*
>
> A print of this film cannot be located.

Música en la Noche   1955, Mexico

> Produced by Alianza Cinematografica
>
> Directed by Tito Davidson
>
> Color
>
> Personal appearance by Katherine Dunham and Company
>
> Contains the following numbers from the Dunham repertoire:
>> *Dora*
>> *Cakewalk*
>
> A print can be obtained through Cinelaboratorio S.A., in Mexico, D.F.

Film Choreography

Green Mansions   1958, U.S.A.
>   Produced by M.G.M.
>   Directed by Mel Ferrer
>   Color
>   Choreography by Katherine Dunham

Karaibishe Rhythmen   1960, Austria
>   Produced for television by WDR Fernsehen, Koln, Germany
>   Directed by Gunther Hassert
>   Black and White
>   Television special entirely dedicated to Katherine Dunham and her
>   Company
>   Contains the following numbers from the Dunham repertoire:

Afrique	*Samba*
Rhumba Trio	*Floyd's Guitar Blues*
Choros (No. 1 and No. 4)	*Strutter's Ball*
Cumbia	*Cakewalk*

>   The print is the property of German Television.

The Bible   1964, Italy
>   Produced by Dino de Laurentiis for Twentieth Century Fox/Seven Arts
>   Directed by John Huston
>   Color
>   Sodom and Gomorrah and Festival dance sequences conceived, staged, and
>   choreographed by Katherine Dunham.

Note: Although Katherine Dunham and Company appeared on numerous television programs throughout the world, most of these programs were not taped at the time, and there seems to be no film or record of them.

Glossary

The following are the definitions of terms as used by the author.

Agwe (also *Maître Aqué*)   God of the sea

Aïda Ouedo   The virgin mother, Damballa's wife

Asson (also *Ason*)   The sacred gourd rattle surrounded by colored beads and dried snake vertebrae used by the priest and priestess

Bamboche   A social dance event, a get-together

Black Virgin   Virgin of Regla, Yemanja, goddess in Cuba and Brazil (*see Yemanja*)

Breadfruit   A staple of the Caribbean, much like a potato

Cacos   Haitian peasants' military corps dating from the revolution

Carnaval   A festival. There are two kinds of carnivals in Haiti. The city carnival, Mardi Gras, and the peasant carnival, Rara. Folk dances are often performed during these carnivals.

Combite   A cooperative work party with rhythmic accompaniment

Damballa   *Vaudun* god of the Rada (Arada) Dahomey cult; also dance term for snakelike body ripple movement

Elite   Upper-class Haitian

Erzulie   Freda Damballa's mistress, a goddess who is said to inhabit the sea

Feint   An open body movement to receive a spirit or *loa*; a break in the movement

Fetish   An object believed useful in averting evil or bringing good

Gris-Gris   A fetish for protection; a sack hung on a cord around the neck containing special objects, hung on doorposts, or buried on the property; said to have magic powers

Haute Taille   High-style Martinique dresses worn at festivals and balls

Hounci Canzo   A second-degree acolyte who has been tested by trial by fire; a *hounci* whose *loa* has been tamed or controlled

Hounci Initiate   A server of the lowest rank in the *vaudun* cults of Haiti, Brazil, and Cuba

Houngan   *Vaudun* priest

Houngfor   *Vaudun* temple dedicated to Haitian *loa* or gods for permanent housing and ceremonial offerings

Koromantee   A Jamaican dance of preparation for war named after a West African tribe

Lavé Tête   The first stage of preparation to be initiated into the *vaudun* cult

Legba   (Cuban, Alegba)—Guardian of the gates and crossroads

Lenguesou   *Vaudun* god associated with exorcism

Loa   The spirit or a god who "mounts" or "possesses" someone during the *vaudun* ceremony

Macarena   Black virgin of Guadelupe, protector of bullfighters

Macumberos   High priest and practitioner in Lucumi cult of Brazil (*see Santero*)

Mana   The spiritual essence of an initiate

Meringué   Haitian national social dance and music

Mount   The god enters a *hounci* body, and the *hounci* becomes "ridden" by that god

Mulatto   A black Haitian with white blood mixture; a person of mixed black and white ancestry

Ochun   (Cuban, Del Cobre)—Goddess of the river

Orgeat   A syurpy drink with an almond liquid base

Ounga   (Also *wanga*, *ouanga*)—A charm

Patois   A dialect of French and African

Peasant   Haitian farming class

Peristyle   Thatched roofing on a small, temporary room used for ritual in a *vaudun* temple

Possessed   See Mount

Poteau–Mitan   The central post of a tonnelle; the *loa* enters by way of this post

Priest   Male leader in *vaudun*

Priestess   Female leader in *vaudun*

St. Lazarus   (Cuban, San Lazaro)—Saint for crippled joints

Santero   High priest and practitioner in the Lucumi cult of Brazil (*see Macumberos*)

Shango   A god of the Rada (Arada) Dahomey *vaudun* cult

Shay Shay   Popular Jamaican dance in the thirties

Tonnelle   The large room in a *vaudun* temple where the main *vaudun* service takes place

Trial by Fire   A *hounci* is exposed to fire and heat and shows no visible sign of injury (*see Hounci Canzo*)

Vaudun   (Also *vodun*, *voodoo*)—The religion of the Caribbean, which originated in West Africa

Vé vé   An intricate *vaudun* ritual design made on the ground with cornmeal or flour

Voodoo   See Vaudun

Yemanja   (Cuban, Virgin Dela Regla) A black virgin goddess

Yonvalou   (Also *Yanvalou*, *Yenvalou*) The Rada (Arada) Dahomey *vaudun* cult rhythm and dance of humility and assurance

Index

Morris, Lenwood, 6, 75, 97, 102, 109, 110, 114

Napoleon I, Emperor, 5
National Association for the Advancement of the Colored People, 69
Negro Dance Group, 27
Negro Rhapsody, 27
Negulesco, Jean, 46

Officer, Marion, 99-100
Ohardieno, Roger, 1

Page, Ruth, 25, 27, 41, 47, 104
Papich, Steven, 77
Pardon My Sarong (film), 46
Performing Arts Training Center (PATC) 6, 40, 78, 80, 91-100, 126
Pins and Needles, 47
Piquion, René, 37
Pratt, Davis, 60, 127
Pratt, John, 5, 45, 47, 48, 54, 56, 64, 65, 71, 109, 124, 127
Pratt, Marie Christine, 64-66
Price-Mars, Dr. Jean, 37, 38

Rara Tonga, 45-46
Redfield, Robert, 49
Reeser, Doc, 37, 82
Rites de Passage, 55
Robbins, Jerome, 47
Robeson, Paul, 57
Robinson, Bill "Bojangles," 46

Rose, Billy, 55
Rosenwald Foundation, 26, 28-31, 48-49
Rosita, Godmother, 82, 86, 88-89
Rouzier sisters, 37-38
Run, Little Chillun (Johnson), 42

Saint-Mery, Moreau de, 37
San Francisco Symphony, 53
Savage, Archie, 97
Schaefer, Louis, 47
Schofield, Paul, 45
Scott, Margery, 74
Scott, Raymond, 45
Sebree, Charles, 26
Senghers, President Leopold, 61, 62
Senior Citizens for the Performing Arts, 92
Shay Shay, 35
Shrimp Residence (recipe), 8
Shubert, Lee, 56, 120
Simpson, Gordon, 109
Sissle, Noble, 68
Skinner, Howard, 53, 57
Southern Illinois University, 60, 61, 91, 93
Southland, 70-73
Speranzeva, Ludmila, 27, 41
Star Spangled Rhythm (film), 46
Stern, Alfred, 49
Stern, Mrs. Alfred Rosenwald, 27-28
Stormy Weather (film), 3, 47